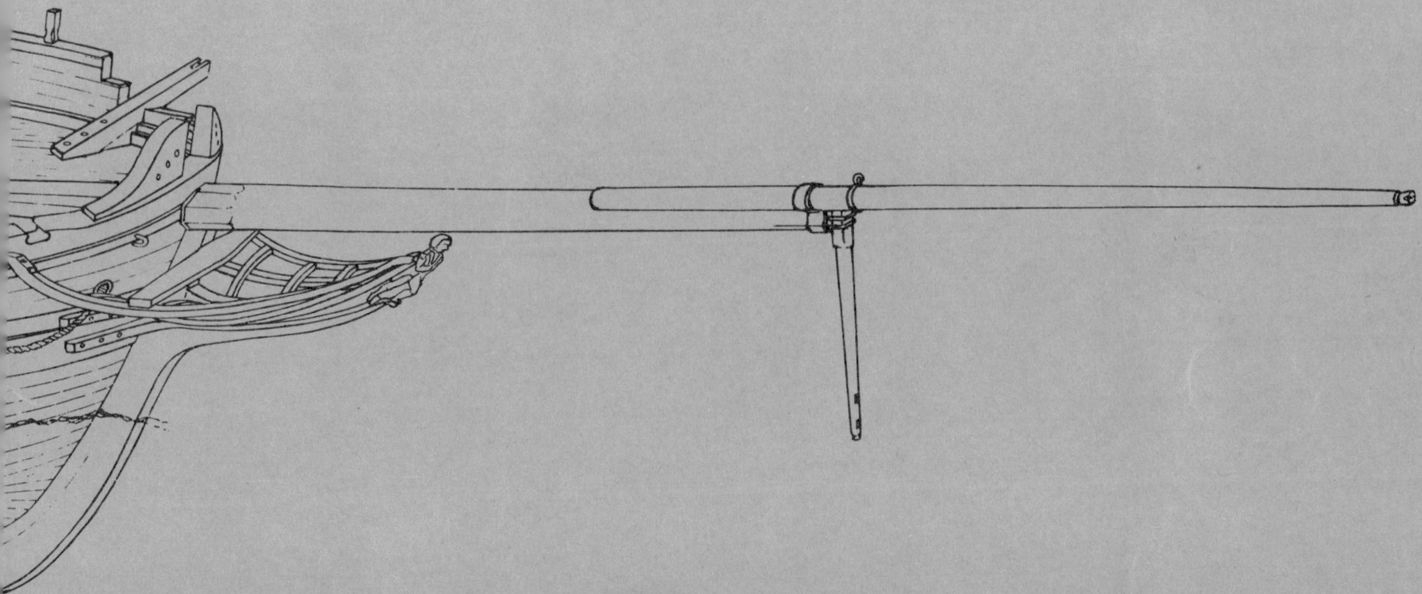

623.8224 Cain, Emily.
C
         Ghost ships

MAR 5 1984

DATE			

WITHDRAWN
Baldwinsville Public Library
Baldwinsville, New York 13027

© THE BAKER & TAYLOR CO.

Ghost Ships

Baldwinsville Public Library
Baldwinsville, New York 13027

Ghost Ships

Hamilton and Scourge:
Historical Treasures from the War of 1812

EMILY CAIN

MUSSON/*Toronto*
A member of the General Publishing Group

Beaufort Books
NEW YORK   TORONTO

Copyright © 1983 The *Hamilton* and *Scourge* Foundation, Inc.

All rights reserved. No part of this publication may be reproduced or transmitted in any form or by any means, electronic or mechanical, including photography, recording, or any information storage or retrieval system, without permission in writing from the publisher.

Excerpts taken from *Hail Columbia! The Rise and Fall of a Schooner* by Dana Story, Copyright © 1972 by Dana Story, used by permission of Crown Publishers, Inc.

First published in 1983 by Musson
A Division of General Publishing Co. Limited
30 Lesmill Road
Toronto, Ontario
M3B 2T6

Canadian Cataloguing in Publication Data

Cain, Emily.
   Ghost ships: Hamilton and Scourge

Bibliography: p.
Includes index.
ISBN 0-7737-0070-6

1. Hamilton (Schooner). 2. Scourge (Schooner). 3. United States — History — War of 1812 — Naval operations.
   4. Hamilton-Scourge Project. I. Title.

E360.C34   973.5′25   C83-098670-7

Beaufort Books
9 East 40th Street
New York, New York
10016

First edition

10 9 8 7 6 5 4 3 2 1

Library of Congress Cataloging in Publication Data

Cain, Emily.
   Ghost ships.

1. Hamilton (Ship) 2. Scourge (Ship) 3. Underwater archaeology — Ontario, Lake (N.Y. and Ont.) 4. New York (State) — Antiquities. 5. Ontario — Antiquities. 6. Ontario, Lake (N.Y. and Ont.) — Antiquities. I. Title.
VA65.H28C33 1983   623.8′224
83-10551
ISBN 0-8253-0169-6

Printed and bound in Canada

Design/ Maher & Murtagh

CONTENTS

Preface 6
Foreword 8
Introduction 11
Author's Note 12

PART ONE
Early Schooner Days on Lake Ontario:
The World of *Diana* and *Lord Nelson* 18

PART TWO
Hamilton and *Scourge*: Eighteen-Twelvers on
Lake Ontario 58

PART THREE
Shipwreck 98

PART FOUR
Hamilton and *Scourge* Found 124

Notes 134
List of Illustrations 144
Acknowledgements 148
Index 150

PREFACE

It is rare that a community is given the opportunity to participate in a world-class project. The City of Hamilton is extremely fortunate in having such an opportunity in the form of the magnificently preserved armed merchant schooners *Hamilton* and *Scourge*. The two vessels, with all their contents, will be raised and displayed in an international-level museum. For this purpose, the Regional Municipality of Hamilton-Wentworth through the Hamilton Region Conservation Authority has set aside a magnificent five-acre site in the heart of a five-hundred-acre park on the shores of Lake Ontario close by Canada's most travelled highway system, the Queen Elizabeth Way, which joins the northern United States with the Province of Ontario.

Hamilton and *Scourge* date from the early days of Upper Canada, from which few historic artifacts, civil or military, have survived. As well, very little of the written records of ordinary life in those times has been available in a way that we can understand and enjoy. In addition, these two schooners relate intimately to the history and development of two great nations, Canada and the United States.

Our city is fortunate that someone with Emily Cain's background and qualifications was here to tell the story just when it needed telling. Her book is a history of our two countries' formative years along the shores of Lake Ontario nearly two hundred years ago. It is told sensitively and understandably by a transplanted Yankee with deep British roots.

WILLIAM M. McCULLOCH
Chairman
The *Hamilton* and *Scourge* Foundation
Hamilton, Ontario, Canada

The striding figurehead of *Scourge* relates to the vessel's brief pre-war career as the Lake Ontario merchant schooner *Lord Nelson* out of Niagara, Upper Canada, owned by the dynamic young Upper Canadian merchants James and William Crooks.

FOREWORD

This is a story, a romance, of life and death in the days of Napoleon Bonaparte, James Madison, and Sir Isaac Brock. It concerns the daily lives of people who were busy founding the early nineteenth-century communities that grew into the large cities and other smaller communities which line the shores of the Great Lakes. These people, much as we are today, were caught up in the hopes and problems of their localities, their families, and their "gainful occupations." But in quite a few ways their relationship to the outside world was much more intimate than is ours.

A foolish statement? Not really. We think that airplanes and television have made the world a "global community," but in many ways modern technology has made the real world remote from individuals. You are less involved with the realities of transportation when you are moved from city to city encapsulated in an aluminum cocoon than if you spent several weeks in a small sailing vessel battling twenty-foot waves on the North Atlantic. Your shopping is certainly less personal when you have the world's goods laid out for you in a department store than if you dealt directly with the person who had himself crafted or imported the few items you absolutely needed.

Again, as far as North Americans are concerned, we are more accustomed to seeing warfare as an item on television than to fearing its approach across the lake or out of the forest. We learn within minutes of distant invasions or diplomatic decisions. In 1807 or 1812, it took weeks, even months, for news of such things to cross the Atlantic. Yet, the results of those events and decisions touched the scattered towns and settlements of the Canadas and the Old Northwest very intimately indeed. The tale of the two schooners, both of which lie at the heart of this book and at the bottom of Lake Ontario, is a fascinating account of how such messages and decisions turned the pursuits of peace into the tragic facts of war around the still-forested Great Lakes.

Emily Cain has woven around these two little commercial vessels a fabric of detail that brings vividly before us the circumstances of their building, their peace-time purposes, and their conversion into ships of war. She recalls for us the acts of gallantry, of courage, and of fear of which they are still the memorials. Not least, she sets them in the context of a society that is primitive yet personal and excited by its almost idyllic surroundings.

That society was, of course, deeply riven by confrontation between the two distant governments that held sway over its northern and southern portions. When Britain undertook to oppose the continental tyranny imposed upon Europe by Napoleon she decided that she must prevent trade with the French-controlled European ports. The resulting interference with American ships on the high seas was viewed by Presidents Jefferson and Madison as infringing upon the recently won independence of the United States, and the end result was the War of 1812. The manner in which the people of the Great Lakes region were enmeshed in this spin-off of a world-wide struggle is the core of the story of *Hamilton* and *Scourge*.

KENNETH McNAUGHT
Professor of History
University of Toronto

The exquisite figurehead of *Hamilton*, which graces the deep still waters of Lake Ontario and recalls the vessel's gentler days, prior to the War of 1812, as the merchant schooner *Diana* out of Oswego, New York. The figurehead represents the classical goddess of the hunt (and motherhood).

INTRODUCTION

The wooden ship is the oldest means of transport known to man. It opened up the ancient world. And, from canoe to kayak, from bark to brigantine, it was the fundamental means of exploring and settling North America. Unfortunately, for those who love them, wooden ships do not grow very old. Ravaged by storms and seas, winds and waves, few survive more than a generation or two to remind us of this immensely long heritage.

Near the centre of North America lie the largest fresh water seas in the world — the Great Lakes. Along their sparkling shores sprang up some of the first and liveliest European settlements in the new world. Made up of tough, pragmatic men and women — soldiers, fishermen, farmers and merchants — these settlements were dependent on the water at their doorstep. The shimmering vistas before them represented their wealth and weather, their pathways and pleasures, and equally as important, something ominous, something that could rise up and swallow them. Unfortunately, these hardy souls, our lake-sailing forefathers, like their wooden ships have been long forgotten.

The dramatic discovery of *Hamilton* and *Scourge*, two 1812 schooners beautifully preserved at the bottom of Lake Ontario, has changed all that. Suddenly the old wooden ships, their sailors and sea captains, and the age that gave them birth, are once again alive.

These two lovely ships, portrayed so vividly by Emory Kristof's underwater photographs, and which are so historically enriched by Emily Cain's text — allow us a vivid glimpse of our aquatic heritage. They tell us about fresh-water seafaring and ship-building when Canada and the United States were struggling young nations. They force us to explore new directions in underwater technology, nautical conservation and ship display.

Like all exciting discoveries, the ships offer us a panoramic view of our inland waters, of our historical relationships, and of ourselves.

DR. JOE MACINNIS
Underseas Research
Toronto

AUTHOR'S NOTE

The War of 1812 was the North American manifestation of the Napoleonic Wars, and those wars were a part of a long series of intermittent conflicts between the European imperial powers — England, France, and Spain — which continued for three centuries until England finally emerged ascendant after the Battle of Waterloo in 1815.

By the British conquest of Quebec, in 1759, which led to the Treaty of Paris in 1763, Great Britain had acquired the Franco-American empire. Britain was now faced with two major administrative problems: first, to oversee the orderly development of North America, and second, to respond realistically to the American colonists' cries for representation.

The American Declaration of Independence in 1776, after a smouldering period of discontent, was followed by open conflict between the thirteen original American colonies and Great Britain. This culminated in the surrender of the British General Cornwallis to George Washington in 1781; in 1783, the Treaty of Versailles established boundaries for the new United States and promised compensation for Loyalist Americans.

The first Tariff Act, passed by Congress in 1789, was to provide stimulus to growing American mercantile power. In 1791 Great Britain passed the Canada Act, by which Quebec was divided into two provinces, Upper and Lower Canada, one intended to have an administration appropriate to English-speaking settlers and the other an administration appropriate to French-speaking settlers. This was followed by a period of rapid immigration to Upper Canada.

The terms of Jay's Treaty, signed in 1794 between Great Britain and the United States, grappled with current issues: England agreed to give up its fur posts in American territory, but submitted to arbitration on the issues of disputed boundaries, damage to American shipping, and payments owing to Loyalists. However, she would not effectively open the West Indian trade to the United States, nor would she stop searching American vessels for sailors who were supposed British subjects.

The purchase of the vast territory of Louisiana in 1803 by the United States from France (which had acquired this territory from Spain in 1800–01) encouraged a burgeoning westward movement, which spilled into Upper Canada.

Meanwhile, the revolution of world importance that had begun in France in 1789 as an effort to rectify social injustice according to new ideas and in response to economic changes had become a bloody internal paroxysm that spread outward into Europe — the French Revolutionary Wars. In 1799 Napoleon came to power and, despite the watchwords of the French Revolution — "Liberty, Equality, and Fraternity" — created a dictatorship. This changed the French-English struggle from an imperial conflict to one that involved defence of Britain's deepest ideals.

Nelson's victory at Trafalgar in 1805 gave England control of the oceans, but Napoleon's victory at Austerlitz in the same year made him master of Europe. The highly successful neutral commerce of the United States supported both powers; Britain and France adopted identical strategies to control American trade and thereby starve one another out: Britain issued Orders in Council, and France, Imperial Decrees.

The resulting harassment was galling to the Americans, although their trade continued to prosper. The Embargo Act passed by Congress late in 1807, and similar legislation that followed, represented attempts at peaceful retaliation. This legislation resulted in a domestic depression with international repercussions, despite extensive smuggling, and the ascendancy of the western War Hawks, particularly Henry Clay, who considered that economic controls were weak diplomacy, and who were determined to oust the British from North America.

His group prevailed and the United States declared war on Britain in 1812. The former was unprepared but nevertheless moved to conquer Upper Canada. This attempt failed by reason of American ineptitude, the brilliant initial strategy of Sir Isaac Brock, disciplined action by British regular forces in Canada, and the defence of their homes by Upper Canadians.

On the oceans, Britain's enormous naval power eventually prevailed after some isolated American victories, and despite successful American privateer harassment: "Free trade and sailors' rights" was the motto of the day.

After Napoleon's abdication, and exile in April 1814, England was free to attack the United States, but the American defence was successful. The Treaty of Ghent, signed on Christmas Eve, 1814, ended the North American conflict.

Lasting results of the war in North America were twofold: first, the forging of a Canadian national identity, and, second, a finally autonomous United States was free to concentrate upon the development of its vast national domain.

Hamilton and *Scourge* capsized in a line squall on August 8, 1813. This map, published in that year, shows their present location by means of an overlay.

The Massachusetts merchant schooner *Betsey* was painted off Naples in 1802. French and British restrictions against neutral American trade was one of the causes of the American declaration of the War of 1812; another stated cause was the Royal Navy's impressment of American sailors. There is no doubt that many thousands were impressed; there is even a manual of the period which tells an American sailor how to survive in the Royal Navy if he is taken. North American sailors were particularly desirable to Royal Navy captains because they generally had a modicum of education, had been trained on the crack American merchant ships, and had not experienced the corrupting and unhealthy British urban slums of the era. The motto of the day was: "Free trade and sailor's rights!"

Ghost Ships

PART ONE

Early Schooner Days on Lake Ontario: The World of Diana and Lord Nelson

"Row, brothers row, the stream runs fast": a view on the St. Lawrence by George Heriot, deputy postmaster general for British North America, who published his travel account in 1808. Note the typical riverside mill, serviced by a ship.

Faintly as tolls the evening chime,
Our voices keep tune and our oars keep time.
Soon as the woods on the shore look dim,
We'll sing at St. Anne's our parting hymn.
Row, brothers, row, the stream runs fast,
The rapids are near and the day-light's past.

Why should we yet our sail unfurl?
There is not a breath the blue wave to curl.
But, when the wind blows off the shore,
Oh! sweetly we'll rest our weary oar.
Blow, breezes, blow, the stream runs fast,
The rapids are near and the day-light's past!

THOMAS MOORE (1779–1852)
Irish poet, appointed Admiralty
Registrar at Bermuda in 1803,
wrote this song after his visit to
Canada in 1804.

THE FRENCH-SPEAKING CANADIAN FUR TRADERS IN MOORE'S song were nearing the Lachine Rapids on the St. Lawrence River above Montreal. They were travelling on the most magnificent inland waterway in the world, which stretches deep into the continent through the Great Lakes. Traders and travellers then conceived of the entire system as one river: "this part of the St. Lawrence" is what one contemporary adventurer confidently called the Niagara River which, flowing northward over Niagara Falls, links Lakes Erie and Ontario; from the latter, the actual St. Lawrence flows eastward to the Atlantic Ocean. A third river, the Oswego (sometimes then referred to as the Onondago), provided a waterway, albeit broken, from Lake Ontario at Oswego to Albany and New York City, via the Mohawk and Hudson Rivers.

During the quarter-century that elapsed between the American Revolution and the War of 1812, trade on these waterways was controlled by a commercial oligarchy whose monetary and organizational centres were in Montreal and New York, with

Mrs. Simcoe's sketch at the Head-of-the-Lake (now the City of Hamilton). The building shown was King's Head Inn. In fact, the view is not so very different today.

strong secondary centres in Halifax, Boston, and Philadelphia, and connections in London, Glasgow, Paris, and the Far East. Yet, the setting for this commercial empire was largely a wilderness. Joseph Bouchette, French-speaking Canadian soldier and surveyor, gives a description of the harbour at York on Lake Ontario in May, 1793:

> Dense and trackless forests lined the margin of the lake, and reflected their inverted images in its glassy surface. The wandering savage had constructed his ephemeral habitations beneath their luxuriant foliage — the group consisting of two families of Messassages — and the bay and neighbouring marshes were hitherto uninvaded haunts of immense coveys of wild fowl, indeed, they were so abundant as in measure to annoy us during the night.

Bouchette had been asked to survey the harbour prior to the arrival of Colonel John Graves Simcoe, first lieutenant-governor of Upper Canada, who would move next year — with his wife and small children, his "canvas house" bought from Captain Cook's effects, and his corps of Queen's Rangers — to found the capital of the province at York.

It is difficult for us to imagine the difficulties of transportation through the "dense and trackless forests." The few roads could hardly be travelled except when frozen in winter. Mrs. Simcoe describes "that terrible kind of road where the Horses' feet are entangled among the logs amid water and swamps . . . [they] plunge to their knees in mud pools." When she is taken to see a waterfall at Stoney Creek, near the western Head-of-the-Lake, to which there is no path, she found the forest nearly impenetrable.

In 1793 the United States owned, by the terms of the Treaty of Versailles, the portion of Lake Ontario and its shores running eastward from the Niagara River to the St. Lawrence. However, Britain retained fur-trading forts at Niagara (on the American

"A view of Fort Niagara, c. 1783." Originally a French fur-trade fort, constructed to control traffic to the upper lakes, it passed to the British after the conquest of Quebec in 1759, and in a practical sense to the United States in 1796 as a result of Jay's Treaty (1794). The largest and oldest building in the fort, the stone "castle," just visible here, was constructed in 1725-6, and is patterned after a French provincial home of a man of means.

side) and Oswego, and when the Pennsylvanian William Vaughan (later a pilot and sailing-master on Lake Ontario) first visited Canada in 1794, he was required to have a passport to go from post to post on American soil. The United States took possession of the two forts in 1796 through the terms of Jay's Treaty. The transfer was amicable. United States Army Lieutenant F. Elmer wrote on the occasion of the transfer of the fort at Oswego in July of that year: "The buildings and gardens were left in the neatest order, and the latter, being considerably extensive and in high culture, will be no small addition to the comfort of the American officers who succeed this summer."

The first large group of settlers in Upper Canada were United Empire Loyalists, refugees from the American Revolution. Many brought their black slaves, whom Simcoe's government progressively took steps to free. There were also discharged British soldiers, adventuresome men and women of English and Irish stock, and numbers of educated and ambitious Scots. We also hear of a Dutch miller at Four Mile Creek near Niagara, but a large portion of the settlers were "late Loyalists" — Americans who took an oath of loyalty to the King and subsequently received land grants. Due to this immigration, the population of Upper Canada grew rapidly from fourteen thousand in 1791 to ninety thousand by 1812.

By 1793, the first hard years were behind the settlers; they had at first been supplied with provisions, and government grist mills were constructed for their use. Behind them also was the nightmare famine of 1788, when men willingly offered pretty much all they possessed for food. Now a handful of surveyors had started to divide up the "exuberantly" fertile land in Upper Canada surrounding Lake Ontario into townships, which were surveyed into a grid road-system enclosing mile-and-a-quarter square lots, which were each in turn divided into ten one-

"Encampment of the Loyalists at Johnston, a new Settlement, on the Banks of the River St. Lawrence in Canada, taken June 6th, 1784."

hundred-acre parcels. These were granted, in huge blocks, by a government anxious to establish British social patterns. Of course, the system fostered land speculation. For example, the Scottish immigrant James Crooks, to whom *Lord Nelson* (*Scourge*) belonged at the time of her capture in 1812, amassed riverside land that enabled him to build mills before and after the War of 1812. He was, in fact, a pioneer industrialist who greatly benefitted by this land-grant system.

Most of the ninety thousand settlers were "on the land," and Mrs. Simcoe describes the first task they faced:

> The way of clearing the land in this Country is cutting down all the small wood, pile it & set it on fire. The Heavier Timber is cut thro' the bark 5 feet above the ground. This kills the trees which in time the wind blows down. The stumps decay in the ground in the course of years but appear very ugly for a long time tho' the very large, leafless white Trees have a singular & sometimes picturesque effect among the living trees. The settler first builds a log hut covered with bark & after two or three years raises a neat House by the side of it. This progress of Industry is pleasant to observe.

But there were other reactions too: "A stranger here is struck with sentiments of regret," said that inveterate traveller and deputy postmaster general for British North America, George Heriot, "on viewing the numbers of fine oak-trees which are daily consumed by fire, in preparing the lands for cultivation."

On the American side, settlement did not come from the lakeshore inward, but rather pressed westward overland from relatively infertile and cramped eastern communities. Even by 1812, the American shore along Lake Ontario was still a wilderness broken only by tiny river-mouth communities whose main purpose was the forwarding of trade goods. The most important of these was Oswego.

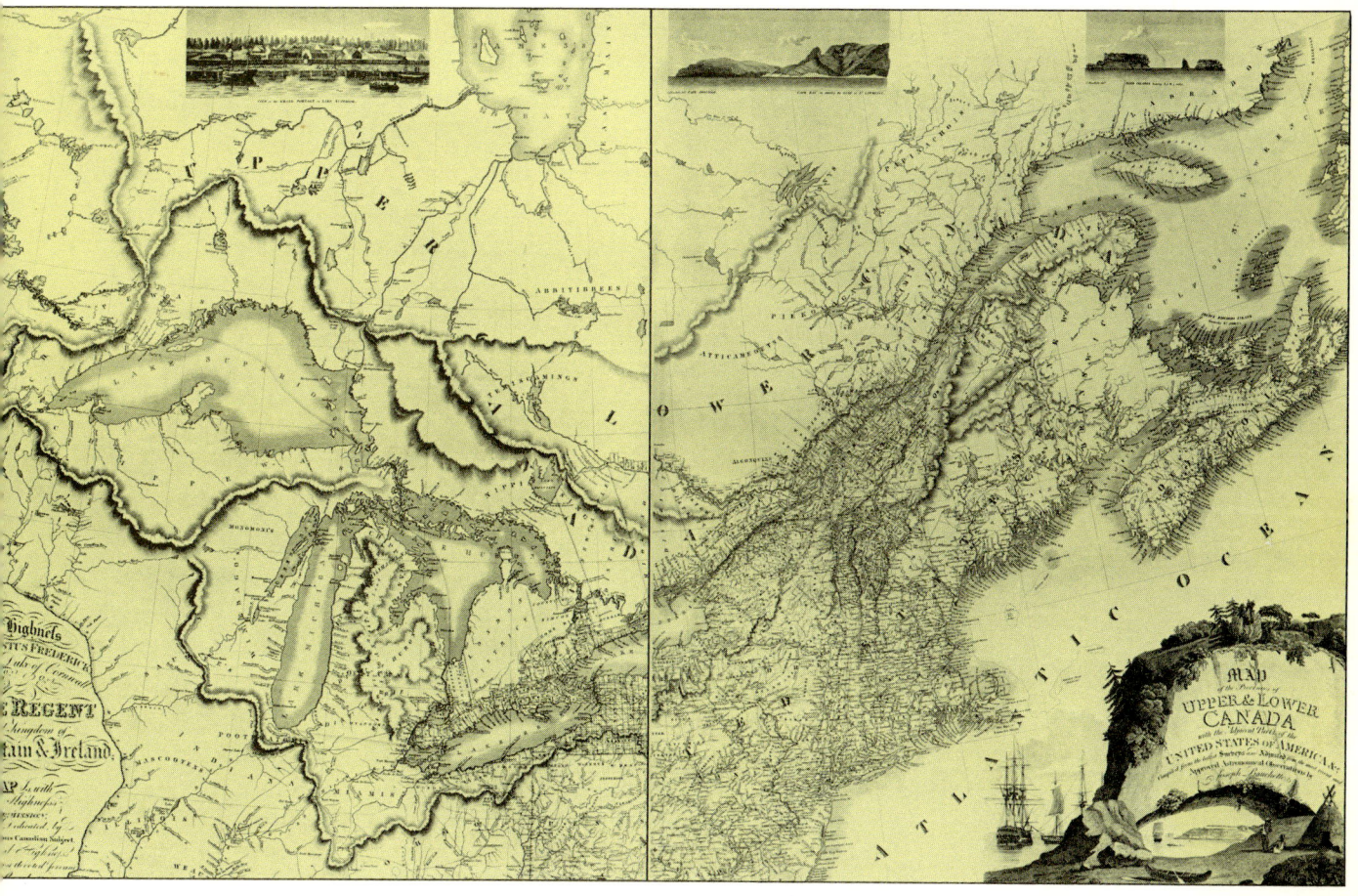

The main communities and ports of Upper Canada were the two garrison towns, Kingston and Niagara, and the new provincial capital, York. These were also provisioning, commercial, and administrative centres; Upper Canada, during the period prior to the War of 1812, and certainly during its course, was administered by British army officers.

Many incidents indicate that the border did not mean a great deal to the successful merchants trading on Lake Ontario prior to the War of 1812. Even for the United Empire Loyalists living on Lake Ontario, the border was only a barrier of sorts: William Jarvis, whom Simcoe appointed secretary and registrar of the province, was a staunch Loyalist who nevertheless sent his children to be educated in New York. He recalled them because of a fever epidemic in that city, and because the schools there did not suit him. His father-in-law, the Loyalist clergyman Samuel Peters, moved to England after the Revolution, but before the War of 1812 he was living in New York State, evidently quite satisfied: "I cannot suppose you intend to turn farmer at your time of life," his daughter, Hannah Peters Jarvis, wrote to him in 1810. "If so, I would gladly make you a Present of 1,200 acres for the pleasure of your company in this country."

Bouchette's map of Upper and Lower Canada and the eastern states, published in 1815, shows the settlement patterns along the St. Lawrence, and rimming the shores of Lake Ontario and "the upper lake" — Erie.

On Lake Ontario, in the late eighteenth century, most cargo was carried by British government ships. Isaac Weld, traveller, tells us that "The naval officers, if their vessels be not otherwise engaged, are allowed to carry a cargo of merchandise when they sail from one port to another, the freight of which is their perquisite; they likewise have the liberty, and are constantly in the practice, of carrying passengers across the lake at an established price." He found accommodation comfortable, and "the cabin table well-served, and there was an abundance of port and sherry wine."

During the two decades preceding the War of 1812, Canada's ships on Lake Ontario operated under the regulation set down by the Inland Navigation Act, 1788. This Act, passed to facilitate merchant traffic, provided for the creation of supervision districts, the establishment of ports of entry and Customs houses, vessel registration with full particulars, clearance papers and dues, and compulsory vessel survey.

In 1799 the American side of the lake was divided into two Customs-collections districts: Oswego and Niagara. The Oswego official (appointed in 1803) was responsible for the immensely long shoreline from the Lachine Rapids to the Genesee River. He was also responsible for "the waters of Lake Ontario . . . lying within the jurisdiction of the United States."

Navigation was then, as now, chiefly pilotage: "Vessels sailing on these waters being seldom for any length of time out of sight of land, the navigation must be considered chiefly as pilotage to which the use of good natural charts is essential, and therefore much wanted," wrote Deputy Surveyor-General Collins to Lord Dorchester, in his report of 1788.

The best rig, in Mr. Collins's estimation, was fore-and-aft:

> Gales of wind or squalls rise suddenly upon the lakes, and from the confined state of the waters, or want of sea room (as it is called), vessels may in some degree be considered as upon a lee shore, and this seems to point out the necessity for their being built on such a construction as will best enable them to work to windward. Schooners should perhaps have the preference as being rather safer than sloops. They should be from eighty to one hundred tons burthen on Lake Ontario.

Indeed, the schooner rig became a common sight on the lake for the next century and a half.

Of the schooner rig, Collins wrote that there would be no need to deviate from it "unless an enemy should build vessels of greater magnitude of force; but as the intent of bringing such forward, or at least the building of them, can never remain a secret, there may be always time to counteract such a design by preparing to meet them, on equal terms at least."

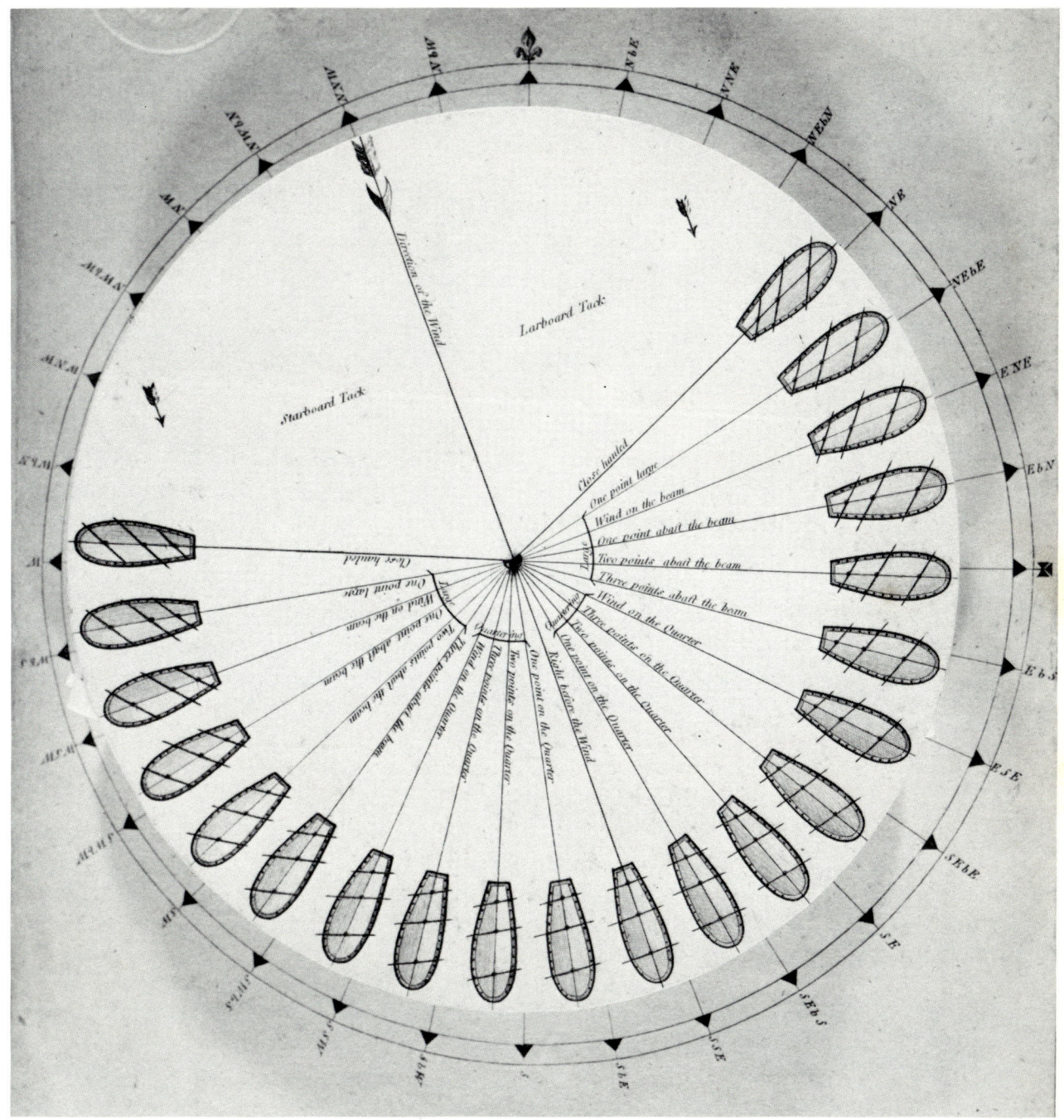

Compass for practice of navigating ships — a late 18th-century teaching device. The lighter circle is loose, and can be moved around the points of the compass to indicate a change in direction of the wind. The ship shown is three-masted and square-rigged. A small schooner, fore-and-aft rigged, such as *Hamilton* or *Scourge*, could "point up higher" into the wind than the ship shown here. This is a safety factor in river and harbour piloting such as that common on the Great Lakes; the fore-and-aft rigged vessel is more nimble and can move more easily off a lee shore.

Sailors talking to Indians at Kingston in June, 1783. (The clothes worn by sailors did not change in the next thirty years; the sailors in *Hamilton* and *Scourge* almost certainly wore clothes along these lines: tarred hat, white trousers which could easily be rolled above the knee, and a short blue jacket. Standard uniform regulations for enlisted men did not exist during the War of 1812 in either the Royal or the United States Navy.)

He goes on to say, "It does not seem advisable, nor do I know any reason to continue the practice of building vessels flat-bottomed or to have very little draft of water; they are always unsafe, and many of the accidents which have happened on the lakes have perhaps occurred, in some degree, owing to that construction. On the contrary, if they are built on proper principles for burthen as well as sailing, they are safer."

Another characteristic of Great Lakes vessels was the relatively great amount of sail carried. The lakes are known as a "light-air" area during the navigable months and, because they are also subject to sudden treacherous storms, carrying a lot of sail could be dangerous.

Furthermore, at that time, Lake Ontario sailors were typically inexperienced. In 1796, Isaac Weld observed that "no sailors (procured from the seaports) are to be hired but at very high wages; it is found necessary to retain them at full pay during the five months of the year that the vessels are laid up on account of the ice," and Mrs. Simcoe noted drily that "the men who navigate the Ships on this Lake have little nautical knowledge & never keep a logbook. This afternoon we were near aground." The situation changed for the better in the ensuing decade, as more schooners were constructed and a maritime community developed on the lake. Yet those first sailors on the lake must frequently have made very good time — Mrs. Simcoe describes running before the wind from York to Niagara in three hours and forty-five minutes: it was "so excessively cold I could not remain on deck & so rough . . ."

Among the first group of merchant vessels constructed on the lake was the schooner *York*, sixty-six tons, built for Francis Crooks, James's older half-brother, in 1794. She was said to have been built at the mouth of the Niagara River, and was wrecked "off the Devil's Nose" in 1799. Two slightly smaller vessels,

Genesee and *Polly*, are supposed to have been built at the same place at approximately the same time.

The ship-building industry on Lake Ontario quickly expanded, and the Kingston area was in the forefront of maritime development. "The rapid advancement of the country in population and improvements of every description have proportionately extended the commerce; the number of vessels in the employ of merchants is considerable," observed Heriot, and "the timber used for their construction is red cedar or oak."

When *Diana* (*Hamilton*) was launched at Oswego in 1809, she joined a small merchant fleet on Lake Ontario: the distinguished American political leader, De Witt Clinton, when he came to Oswego in 1810 as a member of a Canal Commission, observed a total of twenty-six vessels trading and carrying passengers on Lake Ontario, all vessels less than ninety tons.

The commercial network on Lake Ontario was at this time heavily represented by middle-class lowland Scots. They were

"Part of York the Capital of Upper Canada on the Bay of Toronto in Lake Ontario, 1804". York was founded by Simcoe in 1793 near the site of old Fort Toronto. Its population was 336 by 1801; 577 in 1809.

Barracks at York in 1804. Notice the saw-pit on the left: the timbers for *Hamilton* and *Scourge* were almost certainly shaped by a similar saw, worked by two men at a pit.

typical of a large group of Scottish merchants with a modicum of capital who, beginning in the mid-eighteenth century and particularly after the Revolution, developed commercial and kinship networks in North America and Europe. That they saw themselves in an international context is indicated by the scope of the letter that the Queenston merchant Robert Hamilton sent to Simcoe prior to his arrival in Upper Canada. Hamilton's letter was the first strategic move in the merchant's bid for the retention of a dominant commercial power in Montreal-linked Upper Canada; after some conflict with the lieutenant-governor, he was largely successful in imposing his vision. Hamilton was helped by merchants, ship-owners, forwarders, and mill owners who sought political power; their names appear again and again as appointed and elected office-holders in the lakeside communities in both Upper Canada and New York State in the years prior to the War of 1812.

The main trading activities on the lake in the period immediately after the American Revolution were in furs and supplies for the British army; later, retail markets were developed with the settlers' produce, largely potash, salt, salt-meat and wheat. During this period of rapid population growth, the lakeshore communities nevertheless remained tiny and specialized.

The population of York was 336 in 1801, the year in which it was designated a Customs port. In 1803, the collector of duties constructed the first wharf for larger ships, and by 1809 the population had grown to 577; in 1812 the brick government buildings, houses, storehouses, and forts excited considerable pride.

But the wilderness was very close: "There was a great depredation committed the night before last by a flock of wolves that came into the Town," wrote Joseph Willcocks, on November 3, 1800. "One man lost seventeen sheep." In another letter that same year he related: "Two great bears took away two pigs .... They carried the pigs in their arms and ran on their hind legs."

To the east, and at the source of the St. Lawrence, Kingston was the most important community in Canada west of Montreal. In 1792 there were approximately fifty houses; an observer three years later described "about 129 or 130" houses. Heriot published his description in 1808:

> Kingston is charmingly situated on the northern coast of the St. Lawrence. Besides several commodious dwellings, constructed of stone of an excellent quality, it contains a barrack for troops, a gaol and courthouse, an episcopal church, an hospital, and several extensive storehouses. At this place the vessels belonging to government, used in navigating Lake Ontario, are constructed; and from hence, merchandise and other articles which are conveyed from

A View of Cataraqui on the Entrance of Lake Ontario in Canada, taken from Capt. Brant's house July 16 90.

the lower province, in bateaux, are embarked to be transported to Niagara, York, and other settlements bordering on the Lake.

Isaac Weld, in the latter half of the 1790s, wrote that the principal merchants who resided at Kingston were "partners of old established houses at Montreal and Quebec. A stranger, especially if a British subject, is sure to meet with a most hospitable and friendly reception from them, as he passes through the place."

At Kingston, continued Heriot, "there are two coves or inlets, where vessels come to anchor, and on which wharfs are constructed, for loading, or discharging their cargoes. That appropriated for the vessels of government is at some distance from the town, and is formed by a promontory on the east, and a peninsula, called Point Frederick. On this are placed the naval store, and yard for building these vessels. A master-builder, with some artificers, resides upon the spot, and is kept in constant employ."

It was at Kingston in 1806 that — wisely preparing for a possible conflict — the commander-in-chief of the forces in Upper Canada, Isaac Brock, revived the somewhat lapsed Prov-

"A View of Cataraqui (Kingston) at the Entrance of Lake Ontario, 1784." This valuable deep-water port was the site of the French Fort Frontenac (constructed 1673). The port prospered; when it was captured by the British in 1758, there was a warehouse two hundred feet long, six sailing vessels, ten thousand barrels of Indian goods, and provisions, to a total value of £35,000 sterling. Settled by Loyalists and by Montreal-connected merchants from nearby Carleton Island, particularly Joseph Forsyth, Robert Hamilton, and Richard Cartwright, Junior in 1783, the town enjoyed growth spurred by the War of 1812.

William Jarvis (1756–1817) with his son, Samuel Peters Jarvis (1788–1792), both wearing the uniform of the Queen's Rangers, in which Jarvis had fought during the American Revolution. A Loyalist from Connecticut, Jarvis moved to England in 1783; he came to Canada in 1792 at the request of Simcoe and served as Secretary of Upper Canada and Registrar of Deeds.

incial Marine Department and initiated a programme of training in which gunnery was one of the principal subjects. In addition, the ship *Earl of Moira*, of 169 tons and fourteen guns, was launched in 1805; a smaller armed schooner, *Duke of Gloucester*, was launched in May, 1807; and the ship *Royal George*, of 330 tons and twenty-two guns, was added to the squadron in July, 1809.

Heriot also noted: "The house of the deputy commissary, and those of some other persons in the service, stand likewise upon this peninsula. The other cove, much more considerable than the last, is formed between the town and the point already mentioned. Both of these inlets are exposed when the wind blows with violence from the south or south-west, and drives before it from the lake a succession of swelling billows."

Billows on a windy day were a minor inconvenience compared to the rapids on the St. Lawrence, which impeded direct traffic between Kingston and Montreal. Heriot tells us:

> The transport of merchandise, and other articles, from the island of Montreal to Kingston, is conducted by means of bateaux, or flat-

Hannah Peters Jarvis with her daughters Augusta Honoria (b. 1790) and Maria Lavinia (b. 1788) were painted in early 1792 shortly before the family moved to Niagara, Upper Canada to live in a log "hut." In 1812 Augusta married Thomas McCormick at Queenston; McCormick's mother's trunks, which contained house-hold items as well as clothes, were captured as part of *Lord Nelson*'s cargo when the schooner was prized by the United States Navy. As for Maria, she married George Hamilton (son of the Queenston Merchant, Robert Hamilton) who founded the City of Hamilton in 1815.

bottomed boats, narrow at each extremity, and constructed of fir planks. Each of these being about forty feet in length, and six feet across the widest part, generally contains twenty-five barrels, or a proportionate number of bales of blankets, cloths, or linens, and is capable of conveying nine thousand pounds weight. Four men and a guide compose the number of hands allotted for working a bateau. These are supplied with provisions, and with rum, and are allowed from eight to twelve dollars each for the voyage to Kingston, and from thence down again to LaChine, the time of performing which is from ten to twelve days . . . Each bateau is supplied with a mast and sail, a grappling iron, with ropes, setting poles, and utensils for cooking. . . . The bateaux bring down, for the objects of commerce which are conveyed up, wheat, flour salted provisions, peltry [furs], and potash.

From twenty to thirty bateaux are likewise kept in the service of government, for transporting necessaries to the troops, and stores for the engineer department; likewise articles of European manufacture, which are every year distributed as presents to the Indian tribes. There are thus engaged about three hundred and fifty men, whose occupation it is, during the sultry months of summer, to struggle against the most tremendous rapids.

Lumber was another product of the lakeshores, and of the banks of its rivers: "The timber consists of oak, pine in all its varieties, sugar and curled maple, beech, basswood, hickory, black and white ash, sassafras, black and white birch, elm, walnut-tree, butternut-tree, cherry-tree and a variety of other woods," wrote Heriot. He continued: "The winter season is employed by the farmer in making staves for casks, squaring timber, or preparing plank and boards, all of which may be disposed of to advantage at Montreal. In the spring, the timber is formed into rafts, which are loaded with produce."

Near the western extremity of Lake Ontario lay the first seat of Upper Canada's government, at Niagara. (The town was called Newark by Simcoe in 1792, but both names were in use until 1798 when, by Act of Legislature, the name again was changed to Niagara; in 1906 the town became Niagara-on-the-Lake.) This small community was on the west side of the Niagara River, at its mouth. At first, log cabins were the norm for everyone: "I was ten days in search of a hut to place my wife and lambs in, without success," wrote Secretary Jarvis on his settlement at Niagara in 1792. The Loyalist continued: "At length I was obliged to pay £40 for a log hut with three rooms (two of which are very indifferent) with half an acre of ground. I have purchased logs to make an addition to my hut, which will add a decent room to the first purchase." He comments that "Neither age nor youth are exempt from fever and ague in Niagara." By this he refers to mosquito-borne malaria, or "lake fever," now disappeared, but then a feared and common illness.

The following fall Jarvis was jubilant:

> I shall have my family well provided for this winter. I have a yoke of fattened oxen to come down; 12 small shoats to put in a barrel occasionally, which I expect to weigh from 40 to 60 pounds; about 60 head dunghill fowl; 16 fine turkeys, and a dozen ducks; 2 breeding sows, and a milch cow which calved in August, which of course will enable her to afford her mistress with a good supply of milk through the winter. In the root house I have 400 head of good cabbage, about 60 bush[els] of potatoes and a sufficiency of very excellent turnips. My cellar is stored with 3 barrels of wine, 2 of cider, 2 of apples, and a good stock of butter. My cock loft contains some of the finest maple sugar I ever beheld — made in an Indian village near Michilimackinac. We have 150 lbs. of it, also plenty of good flour, cheese, coffee, loaf sugar, etc. In the stable I have the ponies and a good sleigh [and] the snuggest and warmest cottage in the province.

George Heriot gives his description of the area, and of the American fort on the east side of the Niagara River, approximately a decade later:

> The old fort of Niagara, which was erected by the French in 1751 [sic], is placed on an angle which is formed by the east side

"A noble harbour": Heriot's view of Queenston, Upper Canada, in 1805. The large house with the side-porch belonged to the merchant Robert Hamilton. Queenston was at the foot of the Portage Road constructed by the British Army to by-pass Niagara Falls after the American Revolution. It was a busy port.

of the Saint Lawrence [Niagara River] and the vast diffusion of its waters into the lake. It is erected in the country of the Iroquois, and was for years considered as the key to those inland seas of fresh water which occupy so vast a portion of this part of North America. The ramparts of the fort are composed of earth and pickets, and contain within them a lofty stone building, which is occupied for barracks and for store-rooms. . . .

On the western bank, about a mile higher up the river, the British fort is situated. . . . It is likewise constructed of earth and cedar pickets, and the buildings contained in it are executed with much neatness, taste and accommodation. On the border of the river, and beneath the fort, there are several buildings consisting of store-houses and barracks, one of which is called Navy Hall, and is contiguous to a wharf, where vessels load and unload. . . . A plain, whose extent in every direction is near a mile, intervenes between the town of Niagara and Fort George, the name of the fortress already described. The houses are in general composed of wood, and have a neat and clean appearance; their present number may amount to near two hundred. The streets are spacious. . . . On Missisague Point, which is on the west side of the mouth of the river, a light-house, for the guidance of vessels which navigate the lake, has lately been erected . . .

The scenery from Niagara to Queenston is highly pleasing, the road leading along the summit of the banks of one of the most magnificent rivers in the universe . . .

Queenston is a neat and flourishing place. . . . Here all the merchandise and stores for the upper part of the province are landed from the vessels in which they have been conveyed from Kingston. . . . Between Niagara and Queenston the river affords, in every part, a noble harbour for vessels, the water being deep, the stream not too powerful, the anchorage good, and the banks on either side of considerable altitude.

One of the most interesting sights on the river would have been the paddle-boats worked by four horses, which were in operation on the river at Niagara and Queenston, and above the falls at Fort Erie, as early as 1793. Above the falls, in 1799, a boat, possibly the Durham boat, was introduced which, with six men, carried one hundred barrels (the bateau with five men carried only twenty to twenty-four barrels). Next, in 1801, "a Kentucky boat" was under construction at Kingston. It was remarked to be "the first boat of the kind that ever descended the St. Lawrence, and interests all the mercantile people of this part of the country very much." The builder subsequently made the trip from Kingston to Montreal in ten days with three hundred and forty barrels of flour. This type of large flat-bottomed boat was increasingly used for river transportation in the first decade of the century; its introduction had major economic effects. These were only a few of the array of interesting small craft; rafts, river-boats with running-boards, and a range of sailing canoes and rowboats were also in use in the harbours and on the rivers and the lake at that time.

Queenston was at the base of the Portage Road which skirted Niagara Falls. John Maude, a visitor a few years before Heriot in 1800, had found twenty to thirty houses in Queenston. He described the Portage Road, which "employs numerous teams, chiefly oxen; each cart being drawn by two yoke of oxen or two horses. I passed great numbers on the road, taking up bales and boxes and bringing down packs and peltries. Fourteen teams were at the wharf [Queenston] waiting to be loaded. Here were also three schooners."

As for Niagara Falls, it was then, as now, a great tourist attraction. "The falls itself is the grandest sight imaginable," says

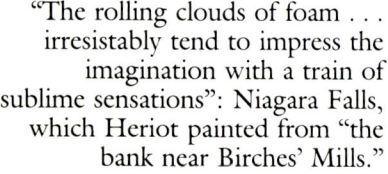

"The rolling clouds of foam . . . irresistably tend to impress the imagination with a train of sublime sensations": Niagara Falls, which Heriot painted from "the bank near Birches' Mills."

Mrs. Simcoe, and Heriot tells us the falls "surpasses in sublimity every description which the powers of language can afford.... The lofty banks and immense woods which environ this stupendous scene," he continues in a description that made its way into a Paris newspaper, "the rolling clouds of foam, the uncommon brilliancy and variety of colours and shades ... irresistably tend to impress the imagination with a train of sublime sensations." By 1806, there were two portages around the falls, one American and recently reconstructed, and the other, on the Canadian side, constructed after the American Revolution when it became certain that the east bank of the Niagara River was to be given up to the United States.

The control of the portage on the Canadian side was held by Robert Hamilton, whose house at Queenston Mrs. Simcoe visited in 1792: "Mr. Hamilton has a very good Stone House, the back rooms overlooking the River. A gallery, the length of the House, is a delightful covered walk both below & above, in all weather." Also at Queenston was Hamilton's store, which was, until his death in 1809, the regional retail outlet of the day, selling a great diversity of goods, stocked in huge quantities: 286 wash-basins; 2,726 pounds of shot; 39 dozen pocket-knives; and thousands of yards of a great variety of cloth: sheet-

At the southern end of the Niagara River on the west side lay Old Fort Erie, shown here in April, 1804, during a migration of wild pigeon. The road is a continuation of the busy "Portage Road" around Niagara Falls.

ing, fustian, canvas. Also purchased from Hamilton's store were such items as fur hats, gilt paper, silver and gold weddingrings, and farm wagons.

Keeping their own store at nearby Niagara were James and William Crooks. These brothers had emigrated from Greenock, Scotland, near Glasgow, in 1791 and 1792, at the respective ages of thirteen and sixteen, to join their older half-brother Francis, who, in about 1788, had started a store at Fort Niagara across the river when it was a British possession. The boys came from a very large middle-class family; the father was a surveyor or contractor involved in the laying out of Edinburgh "New Town." James worked as a clerk in Francis's store until the latter's death, about 1796; James took over the management, and moved the business across the river in 1797, where he acted as postmaster (in 1797 he advertised for someone to carry the mails to York — Toronto). In 1798 he was granted twelve hundred acres and went into business with his brother, William; they built a brewery and distillery and James became a leader in the local system of statute labour by which means the publicsector maintenance of the municipality was ensured. James Crooks perceived that industrial development of Upper Canada was linked to its rivers and streams, and by 1812 had accumulated riverside properties on the Trent River, northwest of Kingston, and on Spencer Creek, above Dundas, at the western end of Lake Ontario (Head-of-the-Lake). In 1811, the date of his schooner *Lord Nelson*'s launching, he was a captain in the militia and lived in a large house at Crookston, one mile west of Niagara; his wife of three years was Jane Cummings Crooks, probably a daughter of the Butler's Ranger who was the first settler and storekeeper at Chippawa, at the other end of the Portage Road.

Lord Nelson's shipwright at Niagara was Asa Stanard, who "in the fall of the year 1810" was employed by "William Crooks and James Crooks, of Niagara, Upper Canada, to build for them a schooner, afterwards called the *Lord Nelson*." He commenced work upon the vessel "about the first day of October, 1810, and continued at work until the month of February following, when he left off work, and recommenced it about the latter part of March." The schooner was launched on May 1, 1811, and Stanard worked upon her after she was launched "until she was ready for sea."

The most important community on the American side of the lake was Oswego, which, by 1808, "was a hamlet of some twenty, or five-and-twenty, houses . . . the surrounding country,

For many years a French, and subsequently an English trading post, Oswego was the scene of Pontiac's surrender to Sir William Johnson in 1760. A possession of the United States as a result of the American Revolution, and at the mouth of the waterway which led via the Mohawk River and the Hudson to New York City, the port did not pass to the Americans in practical terms until 1796. It was the port of export for salt, then much in demand as a preservative; settlement began c. 1800, the approximate date of this engraving.

for thirty or forty miles, being very little more than a wilderness. On the eastern bank of the river was the ruins of the last English fort." James Fenimore Cooper's description continues: "The place was entirely supported by the carrying of the salt manufactured at Salina [near present-day Syracuse]. Eight or ten schooners and sloops were employed in this business, and the inhabitants of Oswego then consisted of some four or five traders, who were mostly ship-owners, the masters and people of vessels, boatmen who brought the salt down the river, a few mechanics, and a quarter-educated personage who called himself a doctor."

Oswego's main export, and currency, was salt (17,078 barrels in 1807), the greater part of which was consumed in Ohio, but fascinatingly, according to De Witt Clinton, the village also was the route by which tea and goods from the East-India trade reached Upper Canada.

The celebrated ornithologist Alexander Wilson, who visited the place in 1804, described the community in verse:

> Those straggling huts that on the left appear,
> Where boats and ships their crowded masts uprear . . .
> Is old Oswego . . .
> Where numerous tribes their annual visits paid,
> From distant wilds, the beaver's rich retreat,
> For one whole moon they trudged with weary feet,
> Piled their rich furs within the crowded store,
> Replaced their packs, and plodded back for more;
> But time and war have banished all their trains . . .
> The boisterous boatman, drunk but twice a day,
> Begs of the landlord, but forgets to pay . . .
> From morn to night here Noise and Riot reign,
> From night to morn 'tis noise and roar again.

Melancthon T. Woolsey (1780–1838) was dispatched to Lake Ontario in the summer of 1808 "with a strong gang of ship-carpenters, riggers and blacksmiths, etc.," to construct a ship for enforcement of the Embargo Act (1807).

The settlers at Oswego were, in the main, maritime commercial people. In 1810, the Federalist ship-builder Alvin Bronson arrived at Oswego to represent the New Haven, Connecticut firm of Townsend and Bronson. He wrote of his trip:

> The road by which I approached the lake at the breaking up of winter was so impracticable that I was compelled to abandon it for an Indian canoe at Three River Point, and allow my ship carpenters to lead my pack horses to the Falls. I had been accustomed to the rude Atlantic, with a good ship under me, but here was a novelty; I found myself in a cockle shell, deeply laden with iron and carpenters' tools, plunging down the rapids of the Oswego River upon a winter flood, with a strip of birch bark only between me and strangulation . . . my aboriginal navigator, with his cool head, quick eye, and strong arm, soon restored me to confidence and ease.

In December, 1807, the United States passed the Embargo Act, the intent of which was to wrest recognition of the rights of neutral shipping from Britain and France by the withdrawal of a service on which they were dependent — by keeping all American ships at home. The first effect, however, was the undermining of the mercantile base of the country at a time when, to many, war seemed likely; the second effect was the almost instantaneous development of an extensive smuggling network between Canada and the United States: Canadians — being British — could ship abroad.

When the shipping season opened in April, there were enacted, at Oswego, in miniature, the scenes typical in contemporary shipping communities along the Atlantic coast: fights, riots, militia troops called to restore order — and extensive smuggling. The Lake Ontario Customs collectors were responsible for the impossible task of enforcing the Embargo Act along the intricately convoluted shoreline and over the many square miles of water plied by a community of lakers who knew one another and the shoreline intimately.

In the summer of 1808, the forthright and enterprising United States Navy Lieutenant Melancthon T. Woolsey was dispatched from Washington to Oswego with a party of officers that included James Fenimore Cooper, then a nineteen-year-old midshipman, and a "strong gang of ship-carpenters, riggers, blacksmiths, etc." to construct a ship for embargo enforcement. *Oneida* was a brig of 243 tons and seventeen guns. One of the contractors for the ship was Henry Eckford (1775–1832), a Scot from Irvine, on the Firth of Clyde near Glasgow, who had apprenticed in the Quebec ship-yards of his uncle. Fascinatingly, his name appears on the muster list of the Provincial Marine on Lake Ontario, 1793. He went to New York in the mid-1790s and established himself in the ship-building business. Among the ships he had constructed was the long-lived *Beaver* for John Jacob Astor. In 1808, he was "present in person" for the construction of *Oneida*; "he went into the forest, marked his trees, had them cut, trimmed, and hauled, and made the frame of *Oneida* in a very few days."

To enforce the American embargo, small numbers of militia were stationed at points along the coast, including a few at the hamlet of Sackets Harbor, and some opposite Kingston. Nevertheless, an "embargo road" was beaten through the forest and "Nature has furnished the smugglers with the firmest ice that was ever known on this frontier," wrote the Customs collector at Sackets on March 14, 1809. His report continues: "There is scarcely a place from the Oswegatchie to Sandy Creek, a distance of 110 miles, but that the ice is good. Sleighs pass at Sackets Harbor ten miles from the shore, and all the force I can raise is not sufficient to stop them." The embargo laws were generally considered void: "There are some who wish to support the laws," wrote the collector, "but they are so unpopular that they shrink from their duty. My life and the lives of my deputies are threatened daily."

On March 31, 1809, *Oneida* was launched, but due to a proposed change in the embargo legislation, she was not immediately used. The following description of the ball at Oswego given in celebration of the launching of *Oneida* offers an insight into contemporary social attitudes:

> Building a brig hundreds of miles from a ship-yard was a trifle compared to the attempt to give a ball in the wilderness. True, one fiddle and a half a dozen officers were something to open the ball with; refreshments and a military ball-room might also be hoped for, but where, pray, were the ladies to come from? The officers declared that they would not dance with each other. Ladies must be found. No recruiting officers ever made more vigorous efforts in behalf of the service than Lieutenant Woolsey and his command on this occasion. At length, by dint of sending boats miles in one direction, and carts miles in another, the feat was accomplished; ladies were invited, and ladies accepted. A difficulty suggested itself, however . . . by what rules were the honours of the evening to be allotted? Woolsey issued his orders to the master of ceremonies: "All ladies, sir, provided with shoes and stockings, are to be led to the head of the Virginia reel; ladies with shoes, and without stockings, are considered in the second rank; ladies without either shoes or stockings, you will lead, gentlemen, to the foot of the country-dance!"

Eckford had brought with him to Oswego a ship-wright, Henry Eagle, whom he had designated foreman. Eagle (1784–1858) was Prussian, a native of Memel, a port on the Baltic (now in Lithuania). He had spent his early life in England, "in

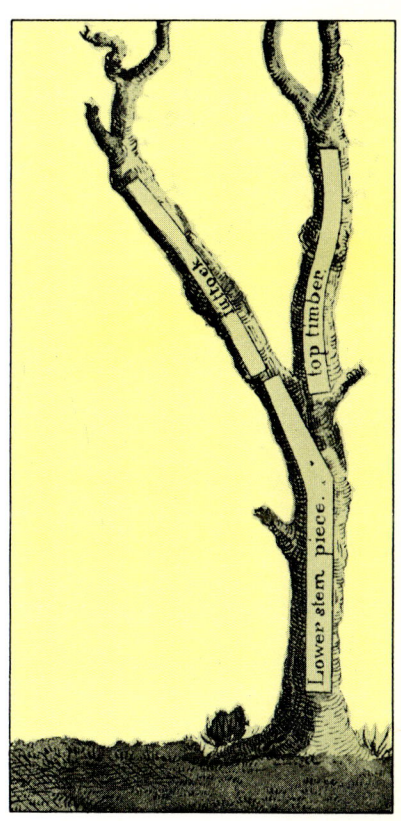

"He went into the forest, marked his trees, had them cut, trimmed and hauled and made the frame of *Oneida* in a very few days." Instructions on cutting ships' timbers from *The Timber Merchant's Guide*, 1823.

The figurehead of *Diana* (*Hamilton*) wears only her quiver and its strap on her left side. Half-clad goddesses were traditional — only they were not usually clad in half of an Empire dress, even in the first decade of the 19th century. *Diana*'s hair is depicted in a style reminiscent of an ancient helmet.

whose marine he shipped." When the Napoleonic Wars broke out, in order to avoid being taken prisoner by the French cruisers he immigrated to New York, where he found work at Eckford's ship-yard. At Oswego, Eagle boarded with Matthew McNair, for whom he constructed *Diana* (*Hamilton*) in 1809; he joined there an active ship-building community.

His landlord, McNair (c. 1774–1862) "of the flaming red hair" (according to family tradition), was an Oswego merchant, ship-builder, and owner who had emigrated from Paisley, Scotland to New York in his twenties, and arrived on Lake Ontario in 1802. By 1809, he owned a house, a warehouse, and a schooner called *Peggy*.

McNair's partner in the construction of *Diana* was a member of the large and active Hugunin family. The Hugunins had interests in the "Travelers' Home," one of Oswego's largest and earliest inns; a Hugunin opened the first store in Oswego, owned a wharf, and worked in lake piloting, and Daniel Hugunin represented the district in Congress in 1825.

The first step in the construction of both *Diana* and *Lord Nelson* was probably the carving of a soft-wood model of half the hull, which gave the shape of the outside of the frames — and therefore the negative image of the inside of the planking. We can suppose that this half-model was small and solid, and that the "lines" were taken off by bending a piece of lead around the model at constant points.

Taking off lines was a complex process, the goal of which was to derive the approximate shape of the outside of each of the frames that lay within the schooner. It was the most critical and exacting step in the planning of the ship, and was generally

The first step in the construction of *Diana* and *Lord Nelson* was probably a model of half of the hull. Full models like this were usually portraits. Contemporary models of 18th century merchant ships are rare; as a schooner model this is thought to be unique.

called "lofting," because it was frequently done in a large, open space such as a loft, where chalk lines were transferred to thin wooden patterns.

But perhaps, rather than continuing to tentatively select from a variety of documentation the steps by which *Lord Nelson* and *Diana* may have been constructed, it would be preferable to present a firmer account of the construction of another schooner, a rival to the *Bluenose I* called *Columbia*, which was built at Essex, Massachusetts in the winter of 1922–23. The author, Dana Story, is of the fifth generation of ship-builders in his family, and although the type of vessel is different, the general steps in schooner construction did not change in the one hundred and ten years that elapsed between the building of *Lord Nelson* and *Diana* and the construction of *Columbia*. Story's description gives us a solid base for reaching back in time to imagine how the Lake Ontario schooners grew upon the stocks in their ship-yards, silhouetted against the wilderness.

After examining the construction drawings to see if any timber was needed that he didn't already have up in the timber piles, A.D. Story took the lines over to Archer B. Poland's mould loft in South Essex where Archie would delineate the ship full-size upon the lofting floor. From these lines he would make his templates of every piece. From long experience as the loftsman for each of the Essex yards, Archie knew what moulds (Essex yards referred to templates as moulds) would be needed first; as soon as a few were done, he would send them over.

Back in the yard, the moulds were immediately taken by A.D.'s younger brother, Edwin James Story, up to the slope behind the

"Beak head" of *Diana* (*Hamilton*), showing the bowsprit at the upper left as it emerges from between the knight heads; at lower right is a hawse hole.

Joining of the bowsprit and jib-boom on *Diana* (*Hamilton*); below is the martingale, or "dolphin-striker". This photograph emphasizes the schooner's extraordinarily fine state of preservation.

Diana's rudder.

Lord Nelson's rudder, like *Diana*'s, has a decorative knob. On the port side (or, then, *larboard* side, i.e. left-hand side facing forward) is a drain, perhaps to handle private facilities for the cabin above.

During the search for speed under sail in the early part of the 19th century, schooner hulls grew sharper bowed, and their masts were increasingly "raked back." *Federal George* was painted at Leghorn (Livorno) in 1798; *Petrel* (built 1815) was probably lying at Sydney, Australia; *H.H. Cole* was built in 1843, at Baltimore, Maryland. (*overleaf*)

Hamilton and *Scourge* were constructed in the middle of this transitional period. Nautical historians are therefore intensely interested in investigating their "lines" and comparing them to those of the schooners preserved in the incomparable collection of draughts of the British Admiralty preserved at the National Maritime Museum at Greenwich in London. These include records of the designs of North American ships taken as prizes, part of a contemporary study of sailing qualities and ship design.

Story shipyard at Essex, Massachusetts in 1920.

Dubbing of *Columbia*'s rudder.

"Dubbing the frames in preparation for receiving the planks. 'To dub' meant to trim each frame with an adze so that the plank would lie firmly and smoothly against it."

"In the case of *Columbia*, each layer of oak timber was six inches thick, so that a completed frame had a total thickness of twelve inches."

"Putting in the great beams that formed the deck structure was no operation for light-weights. Beams were of white oak and crowned or curved upward, to allow the deck to shed water."

"Each finished plank was 2¾ inches thick and might average about 9 or 10 inches wide. Individual planks might be 30 feet long or more. Columbia had twenty-three streaks (of planking) fastened with approximately three thousand trunnels."

"*Columbia* was showing signs that it would not be long before launching time. Her rail stanchions were in and the bulwarks well along; her white-pine deck was laid and caulking started." This photograph in fact shows this stage of construction of the schooner *Mayflower*, built at Essex in 1921.

yard, where piles of timbers of every size and shape were spread over the ground. Carefully selecting suitable pieces, Eddie James traced out and marked the various members and rolled them out where Sammy Gray could hook onto them with Red-eye, the old ship-yard horse, and drag them to the mill. With the roughing out of the keel pieces and a start on the frame timbers, actual construction of *Columbia* got under way.

The big keel timbers were strung out, scarfed together, and bolted, and then the new keel was "turned up." To explain briefly, for the sake of convenience it was the custom to assemble a keel structure upside down. When it was finished, the whole gang would grab it and bodily roll it over right side up. At that point it would be given its proper alignment and degree of declivity and placed upon the blocks and cribbing that would support the growing ship until the time of launching. This operation marked the first milestone, as it were, in the vessel's construction.

The men at Story's erected first *Columbia*'s "square" frames, then the stem, the forward "cants," the stern structure, the transom, and finally the after "cants." By way of explanation, the terms "square frames" and "cants" refer to those members of a vessel's structure more commonly known as "ribs." Through the central part of the ship each rib, or frame, is one continuous member from side to side. At the extremities of the ship, where the shape is finer, the frames are put up in halves, one on each side, and are called "cants." Each, whether square frame or cant, is a laminated member made up of two layers of heavy oak timbers sawed to the proper shape and bolted or trunneled together. In the case of *Columbia*, each layer of timber was six inches thick, so that a completed frame had a total thickness of twelve inches. Frames and cants were spaced twenty-four inches on centres. In a length of 140 feet, *Columbia* had sixty-three frames. With a typical square frame composed of eighteen members, it represented a lot of pieces, all of which had been sawed out.

With the structural framework of the hull virtually complete, it was time to commence hanging plank. *Columbia* would now start to become a real vessel. The shaping and fitting of the planks to the frames of a vessel was one of the major processes involved in wooden ship-building. The planks formed the outer skin, or shell, of the ship and they alone separated the crew and cargo from the briny deep. Obviously, then, it took skill, workmanship, and experience to prepare and fasten them on properly, and it took the concerted efforts of a good share of the gang to do it. Before Willard Andrews and his crew could "hang up" a plank on the side of the ship, it must first of all have been "lined out," or delineated, upon a piece of rough stock. It was then taken to the mill and sawed out in the band-saw. From the band-saw it went to the bevellers, who trimmed or bevelled the edges along the whole length of it so that it would lie snugly against the planks adjacent to it. Lastly, the planking crew could take it from the bevellers and put it (or "hang" it) onto the ship.

It is reasonable to say that the most critical and of these steps was the first one, the lining process, performed in this case by George Weston. How easily and how quickly the plankers accomplished their job reflected in a large measure how well George

Weston had done his. This process of itself required skill and was composed of several steps. It began with George laying out, with chalk-line and rule, how the plank was going to lie against the frames. He had to see that his intended edges were going to be good, fair lines; he had to make sure the plank would not be unworkably wide or narrow; he had to decide where each plank was to be cut, keeping in mind what he had to work with for stock and also that proper distribution of joints and butts was vital to the strength of the completed structure; he had to decide approximately how many strips or "streaks" of planking the finished boat would ultimately have, and then be careful to divide the girth of the boat at its various points so that it would all come out right, with the top edge of the ship not too high or too low at any given spot. The number of streaks remained the same from bow to stern, yet the girth of the boat changed tremendously from midships to either end.

While George Weston was going about his work of laying out the planks, old John Hubbard was going around and around the boat dubbing the frames in preparation for receiving the planks. "To dub" meant to trim each frame with an adze so that the plank would lie firmly and smoothly against it. The frames, as they were erected by the framers, were merely close approximations of their eventual exact shape, the final shaping and trimming being done by the dubber who, each time he went around the boat, dubbed a spot equal in width to the plank that would lie there. It might be interjected here that much of the success of a planking job was also attributable to the dubber, whose skill — or lack of it — made a big difference in the time it took to hang a plank.

It is safe to say that the work of the plankers was about the most laborious of any of the jobs in the ship-yard. On *Columbia*, for example, the planks were long-leaf yellow pine and oak, both of which are among the heaviest of woods. Each finished plank was $2^{3}/_{4}$ inches thick and might average about 9 or 10 inches wide. Individual planks might be 30 feet long or more. In planking a vessel it was customary to cover the lower part of the hull with the yellow pine and to use oak along the upper streaks, where the degree of abrasion was higher. As soon as the bevellers had finished trimming the edges of a plank, the shout "Hang 'em up!" rang out as the planking crew came to lug it up to the working stage. Usually the bevellers helped them do this, and anyone else in the area was also expected to help. If a plank required a lot of twisting, it had first to go to the steam box, where it reposed until sufficiently pliable. Having arrived on the staging, the plank was lifted into place (or "hung") and seized with huge iron C-clamps. It would then be clamped and wedged snugly against its neighbours and "spiked off," which means that just enough iron spikes would be put into it to keep it from falling down; the butt was cut and the plankers moved on to the next one. Coming along behind the plankers would be the fastener, Frank White Story, who bored the holes and drove the treenail or "trunnel" fastenings. Trunnels were locust pegs, $1^{1}/_{8}$ or $1^{1}/_{4}$ inches in diameter, which held the planks on. We might add that with two of these holes to be bored at every frame and with four in way of butts, and with a trunnel to be turned on the lathe and driven into each, Frank White couldn't

Cutaway model (two views) of the colonial schooner *Halifax*, which shows a layout for a small merchant vessel such as *Hamilton* or *Scourge*.

exactly let any grass grow under his feet. Let it be said that, in an average day, a good planking crew would apply from two to two-and-a-half streaks of planking or, in other words, would work themselves around the boat two and one-half times. *Columbia* had twenty-three streaks fastened with approximately 3,000 trunnels.

Planking the outside of the vessel was really only little more than half the battle, for the inside had to be planked, too. This job was started by a second crew when the outside was about one-half or two-thirds done. The operation was not as fussy as the outside, since it was not necessary to achieve water-tight seams and exact fit was not as important.

With the completion of planking, *Columbia* did indeed become a real ship and, with no slackening of pace, work began on the installation of the heavy deck framework. While this was going on, caulkers went about their work of filling the seams of the hull, first with a strand or "thread" of cotton and then with two threads of oakum. Behind came a worker to putty and trowel off the tops of the seams, and following him came the outboard joiners. Their job was to smooth and plane, with their wooden hand-planes, the whole exterior of the hull. Down at the after end of the ship, Tom Irving began his task of making *Columbia*'s big rudder.

Putting in the great beams that formed the deck structure was no operation for light-weights, either. Beams were of white oak and generally "sided" eight inches (horizontal dimension). Their moulded (vertical) dimension would vary from perhaps six inches at the sides of the vessel to as much as nine inches at the centre. Through the middle of the ship they were twenty-five feet long and each, of course, was "crowned," or curved upward, to allow the deck to shed water. Each was meticulously cut to lock into the supporting shelf structure at the sides, and framework for all deck

openings was carefully mortised in. Underneath, in the way of the masts, were fitted the large hackmatack knees imported from Canada.

Columbia was showing signs that it would not be long before launching time. Her rail stanchions were in and the bulwarks well along; her white-pine deck was laid and caulking started.

With the completion of the deck, it was possible for work below to get under way. The building of the forecastle was in the capable hands of Jack Doyle, a man of long experience. It was his job first to help install the big cypress water-tanks and then to build the forecastle floor over them. With that finished, he built berths, lockers, ice-chest, coal-bin, gangway, galley and table for a complement of eighteen men.

There was much to be done on deck: hatch-coamings and companionways to build, rail-cap to be put on, bitts and chocks to be put in, and chain-plates and iron-work for the rigging to be installed.

They put the bowsprit in on Tuesday, March 27. At that point launching day was to be three weeks away.

With an important vessel of such size and depth, and with a crowd expected, an upright launching in a proper cradle was to be used rather than the gung-ho side or bilge launching commonly used in Essex for the run-of-the-mill fishermen. Aboard, others of the men were cleaning chips and shavings out of the bilges; Ed Perkins was hurrying to finish the cabin, and the final coat of paint was being applied to the outside of the hull.

Jack Doyle and his crew melted the paraffin candles to cover the ground-ways. The paraffin would make a base coat for the ways, to which the thick, yellow launching grease would stick. Elsewhere, the gang was taking down what little was left of the staging and removing the heavy shores that had supported *Columbia* all these weeks. The launching cradle would support her until she became waterborne.

After the launching, the masts were floated over to the dock where they were to be installed and hoisted from the water; each, in turn, rested across the vessel's rails while the crosstrees were slid in place. *Columbia* was ballasted while being rigged, and the rigging stretched for the first time, then the second time; the booms and gaffs were hung; and the running rigging set; the iron-workers finished her windlass. After other odd jobs were accomplished, she was ready to sail.

Columbia had a large crew for fishing, but *Diana* and *Lord Nelson*, like similar merchant schooners before their time and after (and until the 1950s), would typically have carried a captain or sailing-master, who might or might not be the owner; and his crew: a mate — the second-in-command; and perhaps three or four able seamen and a boy. Any one of the above might hold the role of pilot. The boy usually acted as cook (although there was sometimes a full-time cook) and he might have been a boy in name only — he could be a grown man, or a woman. Sometimes these schooners carried children, perhaps the captain's family, and in the old photographs we sometimes see a ship's dog.

The crew's jobs required plenty of muscle, especially to raise the big mainsail and to man the windlass by which the anchors were hoisted on board. The job of manning a winch — which lightened the work of loading the heavy barrels in which much of the cargo was stored, if it was not stored loose in the hold — was also heavy work.

Besides physical strength, sailing a schooner also required agility, a head for heights, and good balance. *Diana* and *Lord Nelson* had long bowsprits, which were called "widowmakers"; design changes in the schooner type called "fishermen," such as *Bluenose* and *Columbia*, lengthened the bow and shortened the bowsprit as a safety measure.

Sailing of the schooners, as of larger ships, was typically divided into watches, four hours on and four hours off; the difficulties of staying awake during the night watches are legendary.

A schooner, like any wooden ship, required constant attention. Greasing the great number of blocks and oiling the masts eased the labour of sailing her; rigging required frequent repair, replacement, and adjustment; the heavy flax sails required maintenance; the ship was pumped daily; and a captain who was proud of his ship kept her clean and bright. In addition, re-caulking, tarring, and painting were at least annual events.

While explicit documentation of maritime life on Lake Ontario is scanty for the period immediately preceding the War of 1812, indirect references indicate a sophisticated and even intimate maritime community. Woolsey and Cooper sailed in *Oneida*'s launch to see Niagara Falls in the summer of 1809; the sight of Queenston's cultivation had upon them "the effect of enchantment." After celebrating the Fourth of July at Fort Niagara, they stayed several days at "Newark."

When *Lord Nelson* was captured, James Crooks proceeded to Sackets Harbor with evident familiarity. Alvin Bronson came to Lake Ontario to take advantage of his mercantile connections with the operators of the American portage around Niagara Falls; when that loyal patriot was taken prisoner and sent to Kingston in 1814, he was very soon set free by friends on his own recognizance.

The Kingston merchant Richard Cartwright, Junior (whose communications to his book seller indicate his interest in history, literature, and topics of the day) carried on an extensive correspondence, and his friendships were broad, including the American Federalist lawyer, Customs collector and judge, Augustus Sacket, founder of the lakeside village, Sackets Harbor.

In July, 1811, Woolsey wrote from Sackets Harbor to Secretary of the Navy Paul Hamilton: "By accounts lately from Kingston I am informed that calculating on a war between the United States and Great Britain, every preparation is making for the defence of the Provinces." He enclosed a list of eight American schooners, which, in the event of war, might be pressed into service. *Diana* is on this list; Woolsey considers her capable of carrying eight six-pounder long guns.

Two months later, he writes that Sackets Harbor is "defenceless," and states that "there are but seven men attached to the *Oneida*, besides officers." Sackets Harbor is "within thirty-five miles of the Navy yard at Kingston, a distance that can be covered by a bateau carrying fifty or sixty men in less than eight hours." As preparation for war, Woolsey tried unsuccessfully to persuade American merchants to "lay up" their vessels at Sackets: "The only arrangements offered were stripping the vessels which might be laid up here, their safe-keeping during the winter,[and] rigging them again in the Spring, should the difference between this country and Great Britain be amicably adjusted."

He was, however, unsuccessful: "I am sorry to inform you, Sir, that my recommendations have not been attended to as I should have wished and indeed expected. . . . Indeed, Messrs. Townsend & Bronson have ordered the *Charles and Ann* [the largest American vessel on the Lake] to be laid up at Newark

[sic] on the British side of the Niagara River . . . the Schooner *Ontario* will probably be laid up at the same place." (We can note here that Bronson's politics were "peace-party," or Federalist.)

Trade on Lake Ontario opened confidently the following spring. On May 4, Woolsey wrote to Hamilton that he "was in hopes to have *Oneida* cruise on the Lake, but I greatly fear I shall be disappointed in it. Should you think it proper to order seamen from New York, I think in a short time I could make up the complement."

He continues: "Since the promulgation of the law [Woolsey is referring to the Embargo Act of April 4, 1812] I have not heard of a single attempt at this end of the Lake to violate it tho' I understand that the Collectors to the Eastward clear out vessels for Cape Vincent on the American side at the source of the St. Lawrence as all produce at that place is evidently intended for Canada's market. I detain all vessels bound thither legally, cleared or not, until I have the honour of your further instructions on the subject."

On June 5, 1812, he prized *Lord Nelson*. His account of the capture follows.

US Brig *Oneida*
Sackets Harbor Roads
June 9, 1812

Sir
I have the honour to inform you that I sailed on the 3d Instant on a cruise to the westward. On the 4th (off Pultneyville) discovered three sail to windward apparently standing in for Genesee River — gave chase to them, but night coming on and the weather being too lazing to run in for the mouth of the River, hauled off shore for the night under short sail. At daylight on the 5th discovered two schooners (supposed to be two of the three we had chased the day before) standing in for the land. At 7 p.m. we brought to one of the schooners which proved to be the *Lord Nelson* from Prescott — a port opposite Ogdensburgh on the St. Lawrence, said to be bound to Newark in Canada — she had no papers on board other than a loose Journal and a bill of lading of a part of her Cargo but no Register, licence or clearance, whether it was intended to smuggle her cargo on our shore, or whether she was hovering along our shore to take on board property for the Canada market in violation of the Embargo Law I was not able to determine. But appearances were such as to warrant a suspicion of intention to smuggle both ways. I accordingly took her crew out and sent her with my gunner on board as prize master to this port. After dispatching her I stood off shore in chance the other schooner which the master of the *Lord Nelson* informed me was the *Mary Hatt*, also a British schooner, but finding she had escaped my Line, I hove

Lord Nelson's figurehead is in a standard striding pose for figureheads of the period. Oddly, the admiral is shown with both arms, although it was well-known that he lost his right arm in 1797. He had also lost the sight of an eye earlier in the decade, but this was not immediately evident to observers. Nelson (1758–1805) lost his life at the Battle of Trafalgar which made Britain master of the oceans; he was the most celebrated naval hero of his day.

up for this port in order to take up the Prize and make my report to the Department.

All the proofs which I can collect respecting her voyage I will transmit without delay to the District Attorney.

The captain of *Lord Nelson* at the time of her capture was John Johnson of Jefferson County, New York State, in which Sackets Harbor is situated. Immediately after her capture, Johnson sailed as pilot in the Oswego-built schooner *Fair American*.

James Crooks's published account — written in the third person — of the capture of his schooner, is as follows: "*Lord Nelson* was a fast sailer, and being ahead of several others in Company, beating up the Lake against a headwind from Prescott, the *Oneida* made for her first, intending to take those to leeward afterward, but night coming on they fortunately escaped . . . one of the Owners himself immediately proceeded to Sackets Harbor and reclaimed his property — no war being then declared — nor was it for a fortnight afterwards. In spite of all this she was immediately armed."

The inventory of Mrs. McCormick's seven trunks.

According to *Oneida*'s purser, Alex Darragh, found on *Lord Nelson* at the time of her capture were "some trunks containing dry goods of various kinds, some casks of sugar, Liquors, etc., and six or seven large trunks containing Lady's wearing apparel, which from the directions on the outside and marked within, apparently belonged to a Mrs. McCormick of Queenston, Upper Canada." She was a "just married young lady," whom Woolsey tells us was "of one of the first families in Upper Canada and the wife of a merchant of respectability in Queenston."

In fact, the bride was one of Secretary Jarvis's daughters, Augusta Honoria, who had married Thomas McCormick on the "5th of May (1812) at 5 o'clock in the evening" at Queenston. The purchase of her wedding-ring by McCormick a few days previously is shown in the books of Hamilton's store. The trunks actually belonged to McCormick's mother, Margret, who "in the months of May and June, in the year 1812 . . . resided at Queenstown," and besides clothes they contained bedding and linen: "thirty-six sheets, fine linen, eleven table cloths . . ."

Woolsey states that "as soon as the discovery [of the trunks] was made I wrote to Lieut. Colonel Fenwick, then on the Niagara Frontier, requesting him to send by the first flag which should cross the river assurances from me that Mrs. McCormick's effects would be returned to her by the first opportunity."

However, this was not legal *pro forma*; efforts to return the trunks were Woolsey's gallant preoccupation for the next year.

PART TWO

Hamilton and Scourge: Eighteen-Twelvers on Lake Ontario

"No scheme of defence can be considered efficient that does not provide the means of attacking the enemy at an opportune moment. In the defence of a river, for instance, you must not only be able to withstand its passage by the enemy, but must keep in your own hands means of crossing, so as to attack him, when occasion either offers, or can be contrived."

NAPOLEON BONAPARTE

THE BEST DEFENCE IN WAR IS INTELLIGENT OFFENCE, AND IN 1812 this maxim was mirrored in the thinking of United States Speaker of the House Henry Clay and Major-General Sir Isaac Brock, civil and military leader of Upper Canada.

Clay and President Madison engineered the declaration of war by the United States upon Great Britain, and urged the conquest of Canada as (at minimum) an effective means of relieving the United States from the galling restraints imposed by the British. War was declared on June 18, 1812, and although the War could have been prevented through wise statesmanship, harassment of American ships by the British did, in fact, effectively cease with the peace that came after Wellington's victory at Waterloo in 1815.

Brock recognized that four points of control were crucial to the defence of Canada. These were: Michilimackinac, Detroit, Kingston and, in particular, Montreal. In the spring of 1812, Michilimackinac and Detroit belonged to the United States. In two brilliant strategic moves, Brock engineered the bloodless capture of Michilimackinac on July 17, 1812, and the almost bloodless surrender of Detroit on August 16.

These two wonderfully audacious acts, the latter of which was a battle of nerves and resulted in a knighthood for Brock, gave courage particularly to the large numbers of "late Loyalists" in Upper Canada, solidified Brock's Indian support, and demoralized — with his core of professional soldiers — the ten-times-more-numerous American militia. (The population of British North America was approximately three hundred thousand; in Upper Canada, three-fifths of the settlers were newly arrived land-hungry Americans. The population of the United States stood at nearly eight million.)

An all-out attack on Montreal, the mercantile capital of Canada, would have cut off all interior trade, and would have been the best initial strategy for the Americans. But the United States was poorly prepared for the war in respect to intelligence and organization; its statesmen were sharply divided on the issue of the declaration of war, and initial strategy was *ad hoc*; that is, America waged war at the points of greatest enthusiasm — in the west and on the high seas. The surrender of the American army at Detroit ensured the failure of this initial plan, which nevertheless persisted as a strategy until 1813.

On July 19, a Provincial Marine squadron under the command of Lieutenant Hugh Earle arrived at Sackets Harbor to insist upon *Lord Nelson*'s return, and the surrender of *Oneida*. Earle, who had recently assumed command of the Provincial Marine on Lake Ontario, had entered the force during Simcoe's governorship; his background was the merchant service. He was an experienced pilot, had a good "private character," and, although

United States President (1809–17) James Madison (1751–1836) was a close friend of Thomas Jefferson, who had served as Secretary of State in both of Jefferson's terms as President. As President in his own right, Madison continued Jefferson's policy of commercial coercion to gain recognition of the United States' claim for the rights of neutral trade, and finally engineered the declaration of war by the United States against Great Britain in 1812.

he was short of able seamen (as was Woolsey) and was aware of the shortcomings of the Provincial Marine in comparison with the Royal Navy, that he attacked at this time showed a good understanding of timing and strategy.

His squadron had five ships: 330-ton *Royal George* mounting twenty-two guns; the 169-ton *Earl of Moira*, then rigged as a ship, with fourteen guns; the recently launched schooner *Prince Regent*, seventy-one feet long, with twelve guns; the *Duke of Gloucester*, a schooner, with six guns, and one other small schooner. They arrived at daybreak. Earle captured a boat freighting flour and sent it into Sackets Harbor with his demands.

Woolsey responded with an attempt to escape with *Oneida*, but, finding this impossible, returned to the harbour and anchored his ship where she could rake its entrance. He unloaded guns on her off-side, and had them mounted on the battery; he then took charge of the thirty-two-pounder mounted there.

Legend has it that, during the irregular two-hour exchange of fire that followed, Madam Vaughan (wife of the sailing-master), saved the day for Sackets by giving over her carpet, pieces of which, when wrapped around twenty-four-pound balls, made shot to fit the thirty-two-pound cannon. Cartridges of flannel "made from her domestic wardrobe" supplied the powder bags, and at least one British thirty-two-pound ball was sent back; in his subsequent report to the Secretary of the Navy, Paul Hamilton, Woolsey mentions that he now had "two thirty-two-pound shot thrown on shore by the *Royal George*."

Little damage was done to either side. "I have no doubt," Woolsey stated, "that another attack is contemplated and that they are only waiting for a more favourable wind for the purpose," and he goes on to describe spirited efforts to prepare for this with markedly inadequate supplies.

A major new American effort was obviously necessary on the lakes, and on August 31, 1812, Captain Isaac Chauncey, then at the head of the New York navy-yard (which had supplied Woolsey), was given command of the naval forces on Lakes Erie and Ontario, instructed by the secretary of the navy to "obtain command of them this fall," and to this end "use all means which [he] might judge essential."

The forty-year-old Chauncey had the reputation of a good administrator, and had fought with distinction aboard *Constitution* during the American war against the Barbary pirates. "I feel highly gratified," Woolsey wrote to Hamilton, "in being superceded by an officer with whom I have seen much service, and for whose person and talents I have a sincere admiration."

During the month of September, Chauncey despatched to

GLORIOUS NEWS!!!

York, August 20, 1812.

Despatches have just now arrived from General Brock, dated Detroit August 17th 1812, stating that he took possession of that important Post on the 15th without the sacrifice of a drop of British blood.

Every individual, together with their General, was animated with the most glorious spirit. Upwards of 2,500 Troops have surrendered prisoners of War, and about 25 pieces of Ordnance have been taken.

Thus it hath pleased Providence to crown his Majesty's Arms with an early and important Victory.

Broadside published four days after Brock's triumph at Detroit which was a battle of nerves, and resulted in a knighthood for Brock.

Sackets Harbor "110 carpenters, 700 sailors and Marines, more than 100 pieces of cannon, the greater part of large calibre, with muskets, shot, carriages etc." He noted that the carriages had nearly all been made, and the shot cast, since he had received his orders.

Henry Eckford was the master-builder recruited, and among the seamen was one Ned Myers, who had sailed with James Fenimore Cooper before the war, and thirty years later recounted his adventures to the famous novelist. Myers related:

> Towards the end of the season, our boat, with several others, was lying abreast of the yard, when orders came to meet the Yard Commander, Captain Chauncey, on the wharf. Here, this officer addressed us, and said he was about to proceed to Lake Ontario, to take command and asked who would volunteer to go with him.
>
> We hated the gunboats, and would go anywhere to be rid of them. [Eventually] we embarked in a sloop for Albany. Our draft consisted of 140 men, and was commanded by Mr. Mix.... Messrs. Osgood and Mallaby were also with us....

Major-General Sir Isaac Brock (1769–1812), Commander of the British troops in Upper Canada and administrator of the Province, secured the initial defence of Upper Canada in two brilliant strategic moves: the bloodless capture of Michilimackinac on July 17, 1812, and the almost bloodless surrender of Detroit on August 16.

On reaching Albany, we paid a visit to the Governor, gave him three cheers, got some good cheer in return, and were all stowed in wagons, a mess in each, before his door. We now took to our land tacks, and a merry time we had of it. . . . In this way we went through the country, cracking our jokes, laughing and noting all oddities that crossed our course. I believe we were ten or twelve days working our way through the state, to Oswego. At Onondago Lake we got into boats, and did better than in wagons. [The group soon] reached Oswego Falls, where a party of us were stationed some time, running boats over, and carrying stores across the portage.

While the company Myers was in was carrying stores, Chauncey travelled with the governor of the state of New York, Daniel D. Tompkins, up the Hudson by one of that river's first steamboats to Albany, and thence, "through the worst roads I ever saw, particularly near this place," to Sackets Harbor, where he arrived on October 6.

Two days previously, *Lord Nelson*'s cargo at the time of her capture had been put up at auction. Woolsey had presumed that "no one would be so ungenerous to bid against me" for Mrs. McCormick's trunks, so that they could be bought at a nominal price, and returned to her, but "to my great astonishment I found a party of men who, having no regard for either their own or their country's honour, were determined to oppose me and to run the effects before mentioned up to a high price. In order to silence them I bid five thousand dollars, at which price they were struck off to me." Woolsey guessed that they might have bid against him "from a wish to oppose the Navy which had been instrumental in checking the violations of the laws of the United States," or perhaps "to purchase silk gowns for their wives at a cheap rate."

He enclosed in his letter to the secretary of the navy a voucher signed by himself and his seventy-three-man crew of *Oneida*, relinquishing "claim to the proceeds of seven trunks of wearing apparel found on board belonging to Mrs. McCormick . . . it being our wish that the trunks with their contents may be returned to her and believing that the honour of our country would be tarnished if the crew of one of its national vessels should keep and expose to sale, for their enhancement, the private effects of a lady."

Woolsey expected that the trunks would be sent forthwith to Queenston and that that would be the end of the matter. Instead, the marshal ordered an appraisal of value, prior to another public sale at a future date, and ordered Woolsey to then repurchase the trunks at any price under the appraisal and to pay the deficit.

The sale of the *Lord Nelson* went more smoothly. On October 6, the day of Chauncey's arrival at Sackets, Woolsey purchased the *Lord Nelson* for the United States Navy. The price was $2,999.25, although Woolsey considered "her real value to be about three thousand, five hundred dollars."

Henry Eckford and his crew of ship-wrights, meanwhile, had commenced building *Madison*: "We have a ship [*Madison*] on the stock here," wrote Chauncey. She was pierced for twenty-four guns, displaced 593 tons, and was launched on November 26, after an astonishingly rapid construction period of nine weeks. Eckford's foreman at Sackets was Henry Eagle.

Chauncey proceeded, directly after his arrival, to gather merchant schooners for his squadron. On October 8, he informed Paul Hamilton that: "I have today ordered Lt. Woolsey to Oswego to purchase schooners that are lying there."

At Oswego, Woolsey found the group of seamen of which Myers was a part and put them to work, to equip, related Myers,

Commodore Isaac Chauncey (1772–1840) was given control of the naval forces on Lakes Erie and Ontario in August, 1812. He was instructed by the Secretary of the Navy to "obtain command of [the lakes] this fall," and to this end "use all means which [he] might judge essential."

Henry Eckford (1775–1832), the master ship-builder recruited by Chauncey to be headquartered at Sackets Harbor on Lake Ontario, was a Scot who had apprenticed with his uncle at Quebec. Eckford had served in the Provincial Marine on Lake Ontario in the 1790s and subsequently set up his own shipyard in New York. The builder of *Oneida* at Oswego in 1808, his reputation was made by the brilliant ship-building programme he directed particularly on Lake Ontario during the War of 1812.

some lake craft that were brought for the service. These were schooners, salt droggers, of about sixty or eighty tons. All we did at Oswego, however, was to load these vessels, some six or eight in all, and put to sea. I went off in one of the first, a vessel called the *Fair American*. Having no armaments, we sailed in the night, to avoid John Bull's cruisers, of which there were several out at the time. As we got in with some islands, at no great distance from Sacket's Harbor, we fell in with the *Oneida*'s launch, which was always kept in the offing at night, rowing, or sailing, guard.

The day after I reached the harbour, I was ordered on board the *Scourge*. This vessel was English-built, and had been captured before the war, and condemned, for violating the revenue laws, under the name of the *Lord Nelson*, by the *Oneida* — 16 [guns], Lt. Com. Woolsey — the only cruiser we then had on the lake. Bulwarks had been raised in her, and she mounted eight sixes, in regular broadside. Her accommodations were bad enough, and she was so tender, that we could do little or nothing with her in a blow. It was often prognosticated that she would prove our coffin. Besides Mr. Osgood, who was put in command of this vessel, we had Mr. Bogardus, and Mr. Livingston, as officers. We must have had about forty-five souls on board, all told. We did not get this schooner out that season, however.

It had been Brock's plan to follow his capture of Michilimackinac and Detroit with a sudden blow struck on the Niagara frontier. However, he had been frustrated by a brief armistice that ended on September 8. In addition, Brock's commander, Sir George Prevost, governor-general of the Canadas and commander-in-chief of His Majesty's forces there, was more a diplomat than a soldier and was opposed to invasion. On September 25 he wrote to Brock: "I agree in opinion with you that so wretched is the organization and discipline of the American army, that at this moment much might be effected against them; but as the government at home could derive no substantial advantage from any disgrace we might inflict on them, whilst the more important concerns of the country are committed in Europe, I again request you will steadily pursue that policy which shall appear to you best calculated to promote the dwindling away of such a force by its own inefficient means."

Brock was therefore condemned to adopt a defensive policy, to await enemy attack; and on October 13 the Americans crossed the Niagara River in boats to attack Queenston. This invasion was successfully repulsed by the British army, which was supported by militia, although the price was high: Brock was killed, and Upper Canada was plunged into mourning.

Chauncey's correspondence gives no hint of the American defeat. On October 21 he wrote from Oswego that he was "in treaty" for two schooners, which he expected to purchase for "about $5,500.00 each" although the owners "ask $6,000.00."

"Bulwarks had been raised in her" for protection of *Scourge*'s crew in battle. Shot (a cannonball) still lies in its rack; above, axes handy to clear the deck in case the enemy shot away the masts and shrouded the vessel in a confusion of rope, spars, and canvas. The axes would also doubtless be useful as weapons when boarding another vessel, or repelling boarders.

One of these schooners was *Diana*; on November 4, he writes that she was safely arrived at Sackets Harbor with a full load of guns and stores. "I immediately had her discharged and commenced alteration to mount 10 18-pounder carronades upon her and hope to have her ready in 36 hours." *Diana* was listed at seventy-six tons, in the middle range of Chauncey's schooners, the largest of which was *Governor Tompkins*, formerly Townsend and Bronson's *Charles and Ann* (ninety-six tons). As for *Lord Nelson*, she was the smallest by a sizeable margin, weighing only forty-five tons, according to a United States Navy estimation; the Crooks brothers estimated fifty tons.

The name changes for *Diana* and *Lord Nelson* were announced to Secretary Hamilton on November 5: *Diana* was flatteringly named after him, and *Lord Nelson* was called *Scourge*.

The following day, the commodore wrote: "I have reason to believe that *Royal George*, *Prince Regent* and *Duke of Gloucester* have gone up the Lake with troops to reinforce Fort George," and he resolved to intercept them with his newly formed squadron, consisting of *Oneida* and six armed merchant schooners including *Hamilton*, "mounting all together 40 guns of different calibre and 430 men including Marines with this force. I hope to give a good account of the enemy although he is more than double us in guns and men. His consists of the following vessels as nearly as I can ascertain, to wit, Flag Ship *Royal George* 26 guns, 260 men; Ship *Earl of Moira* 18 guns, 200 men; Schooners *Prince Regent* 18 guns, 150 men; *Duke of Gloucester* 14 guns, 80 men; *Toronto* 14 guns, 80 men; *Governor Simcoe* 12 guns, 70

"*Scourge* mounted eight sixes in regular broadside." Note the tompion, or plug, to keep the interior of the gun dry.

When ready for battle, "each gun's crew slept at the gun and its opposite," Myers tells us. *Scourge* carried enough men to fire one side of her cannons at a time, and this was usual practice. Myers commanded a gun's crew of five. As captain, Myers would have been required to command the crew, point, and fire the gun. Each member of his crew had specific duties, and the rapidity of fire depended upon how well the men worked together. The "exercise" of *Scourge*'s guns would have consisted of loosing the gun from its lashing, and removing the tompion; loading, by which the loader would push a flannel bag of gunpowder down the bore, followed by a shot, and a wad to prevent the shot from rolling out. He would then ram this home tightly. Next, the gun was "run out," taking care to properly arrange the ropes by which the gun was secured, so they were not fouled in the recoil. Now the cartridge was pricked by a wire plunged down the touch-hole in the top of the cannon, and was filled with powder to prime the gun. The gun was pointed, or aimed; and the gun's captain fired it by applying a slow match. He then leapt clear of the recoil, which returned the gun to the loading position. Quickly, he plugged the vent, and the gun was sponged "to extinguish effectively any remains of fire" and the process began again. Notice the cutlasses [or straight-bladed naval swords] crossed above the guns, and the rack for shot.

men; *Seneca* 4 guns, 40 men; making a total of 108 [sic] guns and 890 [sic] men."

Since *Scourge* was to be left behind, Myers volunteered to go on board *Oneida*:

> The brig went out in company with the *Conquest*, *Hamilton*, *Governor Tompkins*, *Pert*, *Julia* and *Growler*, all schooners. These last craft were all merchantmen, mostly without quarters, and scarcely fit for the duty on which they were employed. The *Oneida* was a warm little brig, of sixteen twenty-four-pound carronades, but as

"I immediately had her [*Diana*] discharged and commenced alteration to mount 10 18-pounders [carronades] upon her and hope to have her ready in 36 hours," proudly stated the American commodore in the fall of 1812. The British naval commander was later scornful of the lack of bulwarks in converted merchant schooners such as *Hamilton*: "they have not the least shelter for their men."

Hamilton's 18-pounder carronades are mounted on slides which allowed the gun to recoil after being fired; at the front of the slide is a pivot and at the back a pair of wheels which allowed the weapon to be traversed. The elevation of *Hamilton*'s carronades is controlled with wedges. The weapon would be levered upwards, and the wedge moved forward or back, as desired. Carronades were a modern weapon in 1812. First cast in 1779 at Carron in Scotland and nicknamed "smashers," these guns relied on weight of the shot rather than its velocity to damage an enemy, and therefore the charge could be smaller and the walls of the barrel thinner; the gun shorter. As a result, the weapon was relatively light-weight. A carronade fired a relatively heavy shot slowly over a short range (the conventional long guns fired a smaller fast shot over a long range). The slower shot was more destructive because it did not punch a clean hole; instead, it made many destructive splinters when it hit a wooden ship. Because of the short range of carronades, a ship armed with these was at a disadvantage when battling at a long range with a ship armed with long guns. Note the gun ladle which would have been inserted into the gun and then turned to dump its load.

dull as a transport. She had been built to cross the bars of the American harbours, and would not travel to windward.

    We went off the False Ducks, where we made the *Royal George*, a ship the English had built expressly to overlay the *Oneida* two or three years before, and which was big enough to eat us. Her officers, however, did not belong to the Royal Navy; and we made such a show of schooners that, though she had herself a vessel or two in company, she did not choose to wait for us. We chased her into the Bay of Quinte, and there we lost her in the darkness. Next morning, however, we saw her at anchor in the channel that leads to Kingston.

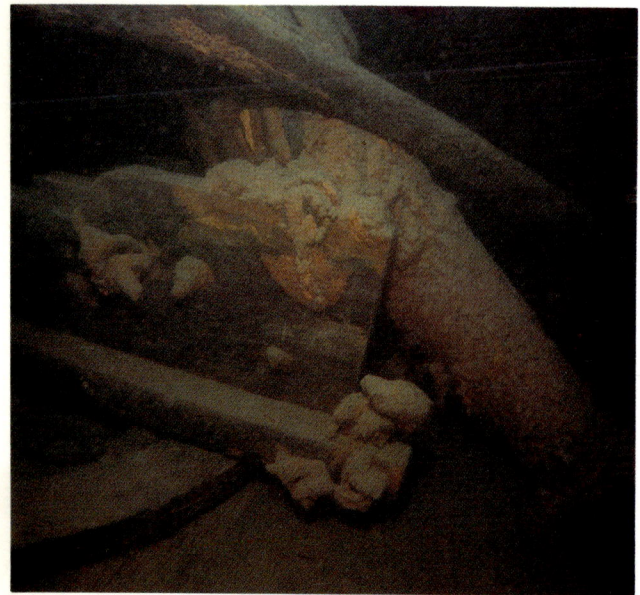 

Hamilton is equipped with this pivot-mounted gun on slides which is listed (1813) as a long 12-pounder. The schooner originally was armed with ten 18-pounder carronades; two were removed to accommodate the long gun, although the eyes which held their pivots still remain. Long guns were frequently combined with carronades to offset the disadvantages of the latter. Note the touch-hole cover on the top of the gun.

In their passage through the Bay of Quinte, the flotilla took possession of a schooner; because the prize would detain their chase, Chauncey ordered Lieutenant Macpherson of *Hamilton* to "take out her sails and rigging and burn her." Another schooner was taken at the same time and used to bait *Royal George* the next day.

Chauncey gave this account to Secretary Hamilton: "On the morning of the 9th we again got sight of her lying in Kingston Channel. We gave chase and followed her into the Harbour of Kingston where we engaged her and the Batteries for one hour and 45 minutes."

Myers says: "The firing was sharp on both sides, and it lasted a great while. I was stationed at a gun as her second captain, and was too busy to see much; but I know we kept our piece speaking as fast as we could, for a good bit. We drove the *Royal George* from a second anchorage, quite up to a berth abreast of the town; and it was said that her people actually deserted her, at one time. We gave her nothing but round-shot from our gun, and these we gave her with all our hearts. Whenever we noticed the shore, a stand of grape was added."

According to Chauncey's report, shot fired at *Royal George* passed into the town, which caused some destruction; rigging was cut away, three of *Royal George*'s guns were unmounted, and she took four shot "between wind and water."

The British viewpoint was presented by this news item in the *Kingston Gazette*, November 17, 1812:

> Early on Tuesday morning last, information was conveyed to town that seven American vessels, full of men, were approaching. At day light the troops and militia were under arms, and detach-

"Pointing the Gun" — the ship's commanding officer has taken over the job from the gun captain; his right hand is on the wedge which controls the elevation; the seaman to the left is levering the gun upwards so the wedge can be moved. There was much discussion during this era concerning "firing on the roll" — that is, the merits of firing as a wave brought the ship up, or as it let the ship down. (Note the seaman on the right, holding a gun's sponge.) Before a battle the decks were sanded to reduce slipperiness.

ments were immediately sent to occupy the different avenues to the town in order to give the enemy a proper reception should they be disposed to land. The Flying Artillery were dispatched in advance of the troops. When they had passed Collin's Bay, several shots were fired by our Gun Boat at the nearest vessels, which they returned, but without effect on either side. At Everitt's Point one of our field pieces opened upon them, the shot from which appeared to strike several times, and they thought it prudent to steer further off. About two o'clock they approached the town and were fired at from all our Batteries. They opened and kept up a brisk fire in their turn upon the *Royal George* and upon our Batteries, which was continued til after sun set, when the enemy hauled their wind and anchored under the Four Mile Point, having done no other mischief than killing one man on board the *Royal George*. It is supposed that some damage was done to their largest vessel, the *Oneyda* [sic], as some of our shot from the Battery at Messisaugoe Point were seen to strike her . . . .

The alarm had been eagerly communicated through the country, and persons of every age flocked into town from every quarter, eager to repulse the invaders from their peaceful shores. The veteran Loyalists, who had manifested their zeal for their Sovereign during the American rebellion, showed that age had not extinguished their

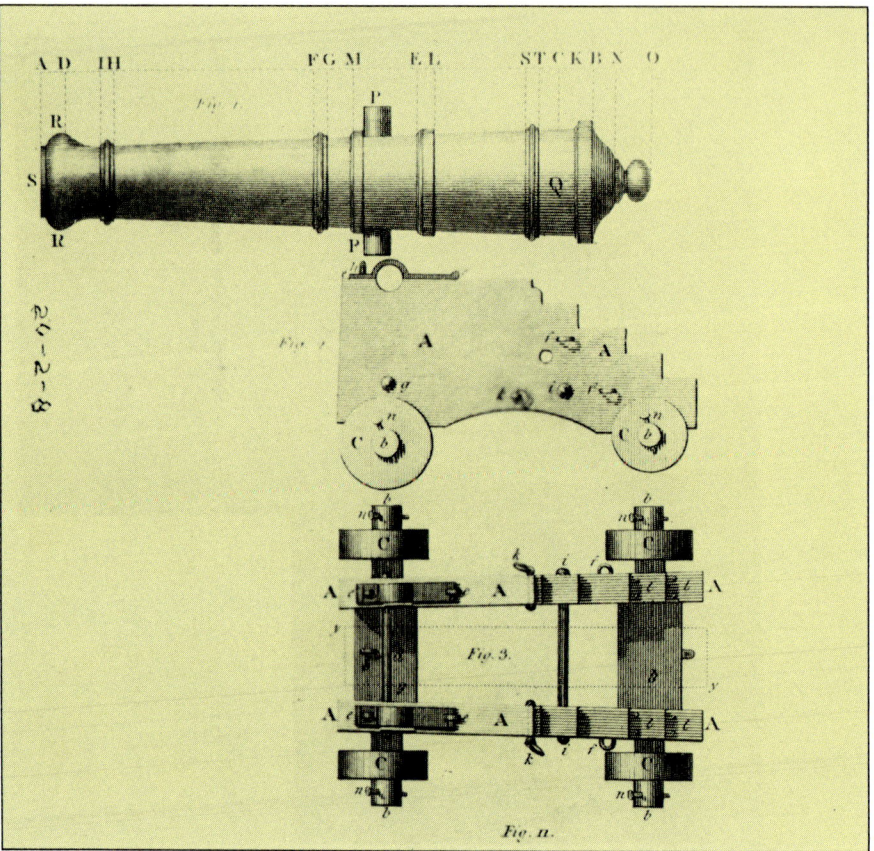

Gun and naval carriage, and "Iron Guns for the Navy" depicting guns of four- through thirty-six-pounder size. According to the Roster of Vessels and Yards, (Lake Ontario, June, 1813), *Scourge* is equipped with four long sixes, and four long fours. *Hamilton*'s pivot-mounted gun is a long twelve; she is also equipped with eight eighteen-pounder carronades. The "pounder" designation refers to the weight of shot fired. The weight of guns on deck drastically affected the sailing qualities of the small schooners upon which they were mounted: *Hamilton* and *Scourge* required great skill to sail.

ardour, and though many of them had passed that time of life when Military Service could not be legally required, they scorned exemption when their inveterate foes approached. Before night the town was crowded with brave men who, insensible to fatigue, were anxious only to grapple with the enemy, who had they attempted to land would have paid dearly for their temerity.

After sundown, the squadron retired; the night was stormy; the American pilots alarmed. On the following morning, therefore, Chauncey "made the signal to weigh, and we beat out of a very narrow channel under a heavy press of sail to the open lake." But, "at 10 [a.m.] we fell in with the *Governor Simcoe* running for Kingston and chased her into the harbour. She escaped by running over a reef of rocks under a heavy fire from the *Governor Tompkins*, the *Hamilton*, and the *Julia* which cut her very much . . . The *Hamilton* chased her into 9 feet of water before she hauled off."

After this foray, Chauncey retired to Sackets, having ordered *Hamilton*, *Governor Tompkins*, *Conquest*, and *Growler* to cruise between the False Ducks and Kingston to intercept ships going in or out. The blockade lasted until the first week in December, and caused the British inconvenience in moving men and supplies.

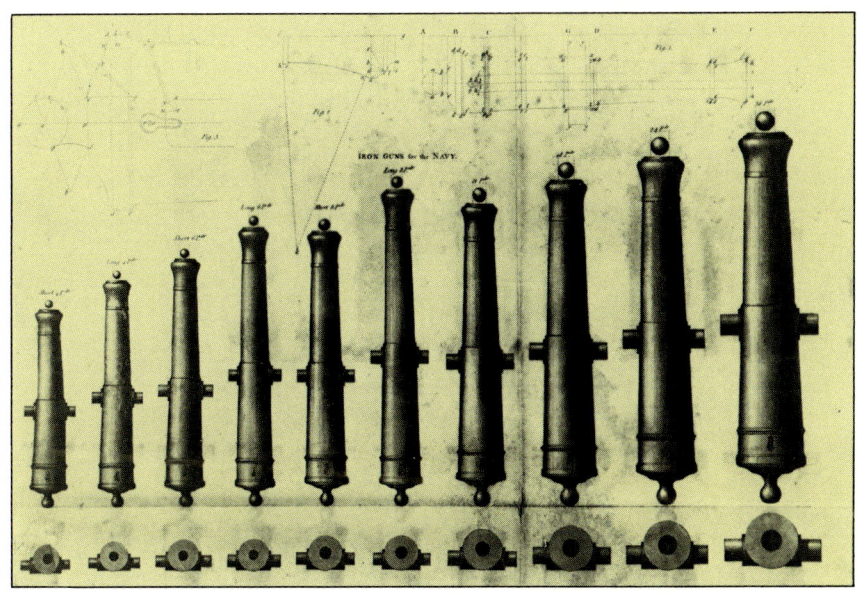

Scourge was outfitted between the thirteenth and the seventeenth of November, and Chauncey indicated that, "I have taken on board guns, shot, carriages, etc., etc., for Niagara for which I shall (sail) the first fair wind in company with the *Julia, Pert, Fair American, Ontario* and *Scourge*."

The American assault on Kingston, with a force pulled together in six weeks, rendered Chauncey jubilant: "I am now prepared to transport troops and stores to any part of the lake with perfect freedom (except from the elements) and I have so informed the Generals," he wrote to Paul Hamilton. "I trust, sir, that you will allow I have not been idle since I received the honour of your appointment to this station." But when the army appealed to him for help, he displayed a caution that would become chronic: "From the advanced season of the year, I think that any expeditions by water would be attended with much difficulty and great danger of the loss of our little naval force. . . . I shall keep in view the main object — that of keeping command of this lake."

Madison was launched on November 26; by December 12 the American squadron was "laid up for the winter and completely frozen in." The fleet was moored in a line flanked by two other vessels that would "protect them against any sudden attack by the Enemy."

Myers tells us: "Around each craft, a space was kept cut, to form a sort of ditch, in order to prevent being boarded. Parties were regularly stationed to defend the *Madison*, and, in the days, we worked at her rigging, and at that of the *Pike*, in gangs. Our larboard guns were landed, and placed in a block-house, while the starboard were kept mounted. My station was that of a captain of one of the guns that remained."

Chauncey gave this description of the ships lying at Kingston and of their defences: "*Royal George* mounts twenty-six guns and is well manned. The *Earl of Moira*, eighteen guns well manned besides the *Simcoe*, and another Schooner. These vessels are moored within pistol shot of the town protected by four batteries and a Block House besides a Canal being cut and kept constantly open all around them of twelve feet broad. In this situation they cannot be surprised. Their awesome guns present a formidable battery of themselves."

David Wingfield, a young Royal Navy officer who came to Kingston with Sir James Lucas Yeo when the latter assumed command of the British lake forces in the spring of 1813, gave a description of wintering ships in Lake Ontario harbours, and we can assume that ships on both sides were treated in this manner:

> The latter part of November, or early in December, all Navigation ceases on the lakes, and the Ships come into port for the winter, when they are dismantled to their lower masts, the rigging being placed in a loft in the Dockyard built for its reception, called the rigging loft, where each ship's furniture is carefully made up, and placed by itself: the hulls of the ships are covered over closely with planks to keep off the snow, and preserve the decks; they remain in this situation til March, sometimes til the middle of April.

Winter provided a respite for officers and men; Myers relates that "The winter [1812–13] lasted more than four months, and we made good times of it. We often went after wood, and occasionally we knocked over a deer. We had a target out on the lake, and this we practised on, making ourselves rather expert cannoneers. Now and then they rowsed us out on a false alarm, but I know of no serious attempts being made by the enemy to molest us."

Wingfield remarked of winter life at Kingston: "From the excessive rigour of the Season, as no work can be done, the winter is passed in one continuous round of pleasure, which makes it fly away imperceptibly."

Local contracts proposed during this winter by the Americans give a glimpse of the provisioning of *Hamilton* and *Scourge*. The navy ration had cost twenty cents per man, but it was thought the price might be lowered by four cents; advertisement was proposed for "good salted beef, Pork, Bread and Whiskey and the other component parts for rations." (Spirits were thought to keep the men healthy, but as Myers himself asserted: "The taste, once acquired, is hard to cure.")

Woolsey gives us a provisioning shopping-list. On March 15,

1812, he had written to Hamilton: "Agreeably to the order contained in your letter I have ascertained the quantity of provisions necessary for one hundred and twenty men to the last day of December next, deducting what is now on hand or already contracted for to wit —

74 barrels of beef
70 barrels of pork
24 barrels of flour
27,500 pounds of bread
1,600 pounds of cheese
650 pounds of butter
2,064 gallons of whiskey
286 gallons of vinegar
72 bushels of beans".

Rations were issued to the men. By contrast, available for purchase by members of the crews in *Hamilton* and *Scourge*, were "slops," or the working uniform. According to a contemporary list, the items of "slop clothing" were generally understood to be:

Common Hatts
Pea Jacketts
Cloth Jacketts
Duck Jacketts
Cloth & Duck Trowsers
Duck frocks
Guernsey ditto
Check Shirts
Com: Shoes
Stockings
Blankets
Mattresses.

Hammocks were also in use, and when Myers was in *Oneida* in November, 1812, he commented, "One shot came in not far from my gun, and scattered lots of cat-tails, breaking in the hammock-cloths." Slops were commonly purchased by the ship's purser, and sold at a designated mark-up; the profit was the purser's. To avoid this arrangement, many sailors preferred to make their own clothes.

Winter was the time for easy land travel. The worst roads that Chauncey had ever seen were transformed by snow into routes along which sleighs and sledges could slide with facility. In fact, if we could look down on North America in the winter and spring of 1813, we would see busy traffic on the supply routes: Halifax to Montreal, Montreal to Kingston, Kingston to Amherstburg; New York to Albany, Albany to Oswego, Oswego to Sackets Harbor; Oswego to Black Rock, Black Rock to

Hamilton's port cat-head is adorned with a carving of a cat's head. This contains two wheels; in effect it is a stationary block; a second block was hooked onto the anchor's ring, and the heavy anchor was lifted from the water.

Hamilton's anchor hangs by one fluke, proof of the strength of her timbers.

Presque Isle on Lake Erie; Philadelphia to Pittsburgh, Pittsburgh to Presque Isle, and back again.

Transportation was a critical factor for both sides but particularly for the British, for virtually all of their supplies of every kind — including Irish beef and English flour — were imported from Britain along the St. Lawrence route. Even the prefabricated frames of a ship — the *Psyche* — were imported in 1814. Both the Americans and British required shot (cannon-balls), powder, guns, and "slops"; and building programmes required nails in quantity — eight-inch and six-inch, double-check; iron of sorts; barrels of pitch; quantities of oakum; huge cables of rope; white paint, black paint, yellow paint, red paint; and thousands of gallons of linseed oil. The oak and the pine were available in the forest, but had to be sawn with huge saws into

The fleet was moored in a line during the winter. *Scourge*'s hawse-hole at her starboard bow shows wear from her anchor cable. Her anchors have folding metal stocks; on the stock one can see the remains of a length of (left-lay) anchor cable. The vessel was painted black and ochre, standard ship's colours of the day. One can still see the brush strokes.

four-inch, three-inch, and two-inch oak plank; oak timbers; big knees; small knees; two-inch pine plank; and one-inch and one-half-inch pine board. Joining required other tools: saws, mallets, caulking irons, and many different varieties of augers and planes. Also needed were tons of canvas in different weights, needles, leather, beeswax, and thread.

By the end of January, the British were building the 426-ton *Wolfe* at Kingston, which would carry twenty-three guns. The ship would be launched on April 28, 1813. Administrative adjustments at Kingston led to the appointment, in March, 1813, of George Record as master-builder. At York, the former Kingston master-builder, John Dennis, was constructing the ship *Sir Isaac Brock*.

In relation to supplies, Captain Andrew Gray, a member of the army's quartermaster-general's staff, which was charged with the supervision of the Provincial Marine, wrote to Governor-General Prevost from Kingston on January 19, 1813:

> ... There is no ordnance at Quebec adapted to these vessels. But as many long 12-pounders may be collected as would enable us to arm the new ship-building here. If we can arm this ship [*Wolfe*], alter the *Moira* so as to render the ship efficient, and complete the crews and new officer the whole of the ships there is every prospect of our being enabled to contest the point with the enemy.... I submit these ideas as it may be possible that officers and seamen may arrive here in time to enable us to act with effect. But if we are to wait til the ordnance demanded from England arrives, the enemy will have the uncontrolled range of the lake for the whole summer, and carry into effect the invasion of this Province with the greatest ease.... It is essential that the cordage for the rigging and sail-cloth should be sent up as quick as possible, while the roads are good.... It would greatly facilitate our operations if some sailmakers were sent along with the sail-cloth.... It may require about eight or ten sail-makers, in addition to what we can pick out of the ships' companies, to make the sails in the time we may require them.

As a result of the Provincial Marine activity, Chauncey suggested that he accelerate his own building programme, and received in reply the following letter from the new secretary of the navy, William Jones, written on January 27, 1813:

> Having just entered on the duties of the department, I have not yet had a convenient opportunity of perusing, with due attention, the whole of your correspondence during the period of your important command. It is impossible to attach too much importance to our Naval Operations on the Lakes. The success of the ensuing campaign will depend absolutely upon our superiority on all the Lakes, and every effort and resource must be directed to that object.

After some gratifying references to the commandant's "capacity, energy and judgement," Jones instructed Chauncey to expand his building operations on Lake Erie.

> The preparations you have made for completing the vessels at Black Rock are well adapted to the emergency; but, lest obstacles should continue to oppose their passage into Lake Erie [British guns were covering entrance to the lake from the west side of the Niagara River], it will be proper to construct a force at Erie, sufficient to insure our ascendency on the whole of the upper Lakes, independent of the force at Black Rock. For this purpose you are authorized to prepare the materials for building and equipping a Brig, of such size as you may deem expedient, in addition to the Gunboats and the Brig you have already made arrangements to build and equip. Iron, cordage, and shot can be procured at Pittsburgh, and I will immediately contract there for as many carronades — thirty-two pdrs. — as will arm the two Brigs at Erie. All armaments and stores, necessary to be procured here at Pittsburgh, can be transported from thence, up the Allegheny and French Creek, in due time to reach Erie before the Lake is navigable.

Chauncey was next ordered to cooperate with General William Henry Harrison — a man of superior capacities. Jones continues,

> This force [on Erie] would facilitate beyond calculation the operations of Gen'l Harrison's army and, in the event of the fall of Malden and Detroit, would enable you to detach a part of your force to Lake Huron, to take post at the mouth of French River, on the N.E. side of Lake Huron; if you will intercept the supplies for the Western Indians which are sent up the Grand River to this post as soon as the waters of those rivers are navigable, and from there distributed through the waters of Huron and Michigan to the Tribes, even beyond the Mississippi....
> This force would also enable you to take Michilimackinac, and command the waters of Lake Michigan. Whatever force the Enemy may create, we must surpass; and with this view it will require all your vigilance to penetrate their designs. The command of Lake Ontario is no less important and to secure this object, you are authorized to build, at Sackets Harbor, another Corvette of such dimensions as you may deem proper. Indeed, you are to consider the absolute superiority on all the Lakes as the only limit to your authority. Immediately upon receipt of this letter you will report to me your plans, requisitions of stores, number and description of Mechanics, and of officers and men ... any particular officers, name them and they shall join you.

The tone of Jones's letter comes like a blast of fresh air and is characteristic of a new American resolve; it also indicates a general shift in the United States to competent younger leadership. This shift was stimulated by continuing failure: the conquest of Canada had not been (as Thomas Jefferson had

In March, 1813, Sir James Lucas Yeo (1782-1818) left England for Canada, accompanied by a sizeable group of Royal Navy officers and four hundred seamen. Just past his thirty-first birthday, slender and handsome, he was ideally suited for command of the Royal Navy squadrons on the lakes. Promoted to lieutenant for merit at the age of fifteen, his brilliant reputation and his knighthood (from the King of Portugal) were the result particularly of small-boat actions and quasi-military assault.

predicted) "a mere matter of marching." It is significant that Jones was still deriving rationale from the westerners. Not until the following year was it perceived that Montreal was the key point to attack; by then it was too late.

Chauncey's correspondence does not indicate that he was stimulated by this panoramic view of his responsibilities. We can speculate that he felt threatened, particularly by the dynamic young Captain Oliver Hazard Perry, whose request to serve Chauncey gladly accepted at this time, and to whom Chauncey assigned command of naval forces on Lake Erie, and supervision of the Brown brothers' new building programme there. As for Perry, he was to find Chauncey a frustrating superior. The commodore was a man whose pride, in respect to his naval command was, at the best of times, easily bruised. This is evident in the seemingly trivial day-to-day details recorded in Chauncey's correspondence during the winter with the irascible Lieutenant S. Angus and the affair concerning the importunate Captain James T. Leonard. As well, the tiffs and quarrels and withdrawal of status symbols for disciplinary purposes ("as I have no sword I beg leave to present you my Dirk," wrote Angus to Chauncey on Christmas Day) presage the deeper problems that Chauncey would have with his command during 1814.

None of this impeded the impressive progress of the American building programmes administered by Chauncey on Lakes Erie and Ontario. During the winter and spring of 1812–13, two vessels were built at Sackets, a small schooner, *Lady of the Lake* (said to have been clipper type and a fine sailer), and a ship whose keel was laid on April 9 and which was the biggest yet — *General Pike*, 900 tons. After she was launched on June 12, 1813, she was fitted with twenty-six long twenty-four-pounders.

Meanwhile, the issue of Mrs. McCormick's trunks — captured on *Lord Nelson* the previous June — was still current. Woolsey wrote to William Jones in February, 1813, to acquaint the secretary with his awkward but gallant bid of $5,000.00. The appraisal of the trunks put their value at $380. The marshal had ordered his deputy to set Mrs. McCormick's possessions up at auction and to oblige Woolsey to pay the deficit should they not sell for the full value. Woolsey wrote:

> The Deputy Marshal has postponed the sale five weeks in order that I may have an opportunity to obtain an order from the Treasury Department for release of the trunks, or an act of Congress for my relief; in either case (although I have friends in both houses of Congress), I can only appeal to you, Sir, as the Head of the Navy Department, confident that you will ever support your officers in all acts of justice or patriotism and valour.

On March 12, 1813, the British Secretary for War and the Colonies, Lord Bathurst, announced to Prevost that he had shifted from the army to the Admiralty the responsibility for the naval forces on the lakes. Although the Provincial Marine had done a creditable job (despite contemporary criticism and despite not having attracted first-class men) of preparing the squadron on Lake Ontario, it was obvious that the job at hand was beyond its training or capacities. The dashing Sir James Lucas Yeo was chosen for the command of the Royal Navy squadrons on the lakes. Thirty years old, slender and handsome, he had been promoted to lieutenant for merit at the age of fifteen. Yeo was ideally suited for the job. His brilliant reputation — and his knighthood — were the result particularly of successful small-boat actions and military assault. He was free because he had run his ship, the *Southampton*, and her prize, aground on an uncharted rock. This event, and the subsequent court-martial (by which he had been, however, exonerated), perhaps made him uncharacteristically cautious in his lakes command. In March, 1813, he left England for Canada, accompanied by Royal Navy officers — among them Wingfield — and four hundred seamen.

Lord Bathurst's letter to Prevost announcing the change indicates — through administrative asides — the vast domain for which the former was responsible and implies the duration and magnitude of the imperial conflict in which Britain was involved. This communication first observes that,

> The faint attempt made by the American army on the frontiers of Lower Canada, terminating as it had done in a disastrous retreat, appears to me sufficiently to indicate the Upper Province as that against which their principal attempts will hereafter be made. Under this impression I cannot but express a hope that you may have been enabled to make such detachments to the Upper Province as to meet the corresponding efforts of the enemy.... 550 men of the 19th Dragoons have been ordered for service in Canada, and will sail from Cork in company with the infantry as per margin, and 150 horses.... Long continuance of westerly winds has prevented the transports for the conveyance of the two regiments from Barbados to Canada from proceeding to the West Indies, and you must consequently be prepared to expect a delay in their arrival at Quebec.... One of the regiments, from the Mediterranean, which I mentioned in my former despatch, is, however, arrived at Cadiz, and will at the end of this month be on the passage to the St. Lawrence. The other regiment, from Malta, may also be looked for at any early period.

The letter continues with a description of supplies:

> The Woolwich troop ship . . . has on board such naval stores as are considered necessary for the equipment of the two new vessels building on Lake Ontario. The carronades required for these vessels, together with the barrack, marine and batteaux stores . . . are now shipping on board a transport which will proceed with the first fleet. I fear that the want of detailed explanation as to the size or description of these vessels may occasion the omission of some perhaps very necessary articles. But I trust this deficiency will be obviated by the directions which have been given to the dockyard at Halifax to afford you on all occasions such assistance as is consistent with the means placed at their disposal.... I cannot ... avoid regretting that the Commissary General should on the eve of a deficient supply of flour in Canada have thought it prudent to export so considerable a quantity of that article to the Peninsula at the close of last year, and I must impress upon you the importance of deriving as far as possible from other quarters than Great Britain such further supplies as may be required for the subsistence of the troops or the inhabitants.

Yeo is to report to "the Lords Commissioners of the Admiralty on all subjects connected with that branch of the service" and

> to remove any doubt which might otherwise exist respecting the nature and limits of the command to be exercised by the naval officer on the lakes, it is my intention to transmit to you by the earliest opportunity a copy of the instructions which will be given on this subject to Sir James L. Yeo, and have only to express my confident expectation that as he is to be placed by these instructions as much under your control as is consistent with the rules of the department under which he is now immediately acting, so you will find him always ready effectually to forward any objects which you may have in view for the defence of the provinces under your charge.

In the same month — March, 1813 — Chauncey's strategy for the season's campaign on Lake Ontario was agreed upon; instead of attacking Kingston, as he had planned, and as the British confidently expected, and which would have caught the fleet during organizational changes, Chauncey would transport the enfeebled General Dearborn's army first to attack York, and next to attack Fort George; subsequent attention would be focused on Lake Erie. Strategic merit aside, both operations provide an interesting view of the use, in naval warfare, of small schooners such as *Hamilton* and *Scourge* for transport, and to cover army landings.

By April 19, ice had finally disappeared from Sackets Harbor, and some seventeen hundred troops were embarked in *Madison*, *Oneida*, and the schooners; on the twenty-fourth the expedition started, but not more than half of the troops could get below at one time; due to stormy weather, *Madison* — which carried six-hundred people — sprung her main topsail yard, and *Hamilton* lost her fore-gaff. The ships were all dangerously low in the water and Chauncey was forced to bring his squadron back to Sackets.

Myers relates:

> The Lake was fit to navigate about the middle of April. Somewhere about the 22nd the soldiers began to embark, to the number of 1,700 men. A company came on board the *Scourge*, and they filled us chock-a-block. It came on to blow and we were obliged to keep these poor fellows, cramped as we were, most of the time on deck, exposed to rain and storm. On the 25th we got out, rather a showy force altogether, though there was not much service in our small craft. We had a ship, a brig, and twelve schooners, fourteen sail in all. The next morning we were off Little York, having sailed with a fair wind. All hands anchored about a mile from the beach. I volunteered to go in a boat, to carry soldiers ashore. Each of us

"A hot shot cut all the pikes from the main boom." Evidently stored in the same place some three months later when the ship went down, the pikes have now fallen and lie across *Scourge*'s hatch opening directly behind the main mast. Pikes were long poles with metal tips which were useful for bashing or sticking into one's enemy. Cutlasses are stuck handily into *Scourge*'s bilge pumps. (The pump spear, or long bar connecting the handle — missing here — with the pump box below, is visible beside the near cutlass.) On the side of the wooden pump is its outlet for bilge water. Directly in front of the pumps is *Scourge*'s mainmast which is prevented from turning by its octagonal shape as it meets the deck. Cleats for halyards are attached to the mast.

A hot shot was a cannon ball which had been heated just enough so it would cause to catch fire any wood in which it imbedded itself; but not so much that it changed shape and could not be aimed.

brought across the lake two of these boats in tow, but we had lost one of ours, dragging her after us in a staggering breeze. I got into the one that was left, and we put half our soldiers in her, and shoved off. We had little or no order in landing, each boat pulling as hard as she could. The English blasted away at us, concealed in a wood, and our men fired back again from the boat.

Myers describes the poor condition of the army:

I never was more disappointed in men, than I was in the soldiers. They were mostly tall, pale-looking Yankees, half dead with sickness and the bad weather — so mealy, indeed, that half of them could not take their grog, which, by this time, I had got to think a bad sign. As soon as they got near the enemy, however, they became wide awake, pointed out to each other where to aim, and many of them actually jumped into the water in order to get the sooner ashore. No men could have behaved better, for I confess frankly I did not like the work at all. It is no fun to pull under a sharp fire, with one's back to his enemy, and nothing but an oar to amuse himself with. The shot flew pretty thick, and two of our oars were split. This was all done with musketry, no heavy guns being used at this place. I landed twice in this way, but the danger was principally in the first affair.

When we got back to the schooner, we found her lifting her anchors. Several of the smaller craft were now ordered up the bay, to open on the batteries nearer to the town. We were third from the van, and we all anchored within canister range. We heard a magazine blow up, as we stood in, and this brought three cheers from us. We now had some sharp work with the batteries, keeping up a steady fire. The schooner ahead of us had to cut, and she shifted her berth outside of us. The leading schooner, however, held on. In the midst of all of it, we heard cheers down the line, and presently we saw the commodore pulling in among us in his gig. He came on board us, and we greeted him with three cheers. While he was on the quarter-deck, a hot shot struck the upper part of the after-port, cut all the boarding-pikes adrift from the main-boom. . . . Two of the trucks of the gun we were fighting had been carried away, and I determined to shift over its opposite. My crew were five strapping fellows. . . . Shoving the disabled gun out of the way, these chaps crossed the deck, unhooked the breechings and gun-tackles, raised the piece from the deck, and placed it in the vacant port. The commodore commended us and called out, "That is quick work, my lads!" In less than three minutes, I am certain, we were playing on the enemy with the fresh gun.

As for the old man, he pulled through the fire as coolly as if it were only a snow-balling scrape, though many a poor fellow lost the number of his mess in the boats that day. When he left us, we cheered him again. He had not left us long, before we heard an awful explosion on shore. Stones as big as my two fists fell on board of us, though nobody was hurt by them. We cheered, thinking some dire calamity had befallen the enemy. The firing ceased soon after this explosion, though one English gun held on, under the bank, for some little time.

"In the midst of it all, we heard cheers down the line, and presently we saw the commodore pulling in among us, in his gig. He came on board us . . ." *Scourge* has these side-steps on her starboard side; the two metal posts supported parallel lines for hand-grips. It is supposed that the unusual hole was used to secure a boat hook; however, some authorities consider that the keyhole is, instead, a sweep-port.

The spectacular firing — by order of Brock's successor, Major General Sir Roger Hale Sheaffe — of the York magazine containing two hundred barrels of gunpowder killed, among others, the American general and explorer Zebulon Pike (of Pike's Peak fame). The British regular force sensibly retreated towards Kingston; subsequently, the town of York surrendered.

During the three-day occupation of York, *Sir Isaac Brock*, the thirty-gun ship, was burned on the stocks; *Duke of Gloucester* was captured; and the Americans either destroyed or brought away with them a large quantity of stores, including a marquee which was made into a topsail for *Scourge*.

"Our troops had lost near three hundred men in the attack, the wounded included," related Myers accurately, "and as a great many of these green soldiers were now sick from exposure, the army was much reduced in force." As for the British regulars, they left sixty-two killed and seventy-six wounded. Five Upper Canadians died while fighting or in the explosion, and five others were wounded.

The American troops were re-embarked on May 1 to sail for Fort George; however, they were trapped until the seventh of May by a spring storm: "The wind which has been moderate from the Eastward," wrote Chauncey, "increased to a gale, accompanied with rain and continued to blow very heavy . . . we have been riding ever since with two anchors ahead and lower Yard and Top Gallant masts down and there is every appearance of its continuing . . . our own troops are becoming

The Navy Yard for the Upper Great Lakes at Amherstburg, July, 1813. *Detroit* is on the stocks; she was launched later in the same month. *Queen Charlotte* is sailing up the river with *General Hunter* in the background.

Death of the American General Zebulon Pike (1779–1813) during the explosion of the battery at York on April 27, 1813. An explorer, for whom Pike's Peak was named, Pike is best remembered for his travel accounts of the American West.

sickly, crowded as they are on board the Small vessels, where not more than one-half can get below at one time, they are not only exposed to the rain, but the Sea makes a fair break over them."

On the eighth of May "We got underway," Myers tells us, "and crossed the lake, landing the soldiers a few miles to the eastward of Fort Niagara. Our schooner now went to [Sackets] Harbor, along with the commodore, though some of the craft remained near the head of the lake."

Chauncey reported from Sackets on the eleventh that, "I have this moment anchored with the *Madison, Fair American, Hamilton, Julia, Growler, Asp, Raven,* and the prize schooner — *Duke of Gloucester* — the *Oneida, Ontario, Scourge* and *Pert* I have ordered to Oswego to take on board Stores which have arrived there from New York and which the Fleet are much in need of. The *Governor Tompkins* and *Conquest* I left at Niagara to proceed up to the head of the Lake."

Subsequent to his arrival at Sackets, relates Myers, "we took in another lot of soldiers, placed two more large batteaux in tow, and sailed for the army again."

When Woolsey returned to Sackets Harbor on May 11, after the attack on York, he discovered that, in his absence, the deputy marshal at Sackets had put Mrs. McCormick's trunks up for auction once more. "They were," Woolsey wrote to the secretary of the navy on May 12, "struck off to friends whom I had engaged to purchase for me at the full amount of the apprizement." Woolsey did not manage to return Mrs. McCormick's possessions until after the war. In 1815, one trunk "containing a variety of articles which have been saved from the general wreck," was returned to her at Montreal.

Before Chauncey left for Niagara, "hoping to obtain the true situation of the Enemy's vessels at Kingston," he sent a flag of truce to Kingston by the *Lady of the Lake* with "Lieutenant M.L. Green of the *Royal George*," prisoner on his parole, and two seamen, who reported that *"Royal George, Earl of Moira, Prince Regent* and the *Simcoe* were ready for sea and that the new ship [*Wolfe*] had her lower masts in and rigging and tops overhead and apparently nearly ready in other respects."

Because of the evident readiness of the British fleet, Chauncey stayed behind at Sackets with *Madison* and *Lady of the Lake*, while the remainder of the American squadron boarded a thousand troops and set off for Niagara on 16 May. That day, Yeo arrived in Kingston via Montreal with "one hundred and fifty of the officers and seamen under my command: the remainder have also arrived." He was not impressed by what he saw: "The ships and vessels were in a very weak state," he reported. "The *Royal George* had 18 32-pounder carronades; the *Beresford* (ex-*Prince Regent*), 10 12-pounder carronades and two long six-pounder guns; the *Wolfe* was launched but not decked or rigged, nor any guns on board."

Yeo began to organize immediately, realizing that "the possession of Upper Canada must depend on whoever can maintain the naval superiority of Lake Ontario." He asked for reinforcements, and (perhaps in order to exert pressure upon his superiors) gave an overly positive picture of American mobility: "the enemy, from their proximity to New York, can obtain any supply of men or stores at a few hours' notice."

Upon Yeo's arrival, the gallant Captain James Heriot Barclay, who had been the first Royal Navy officer to arrive on the lakes in 1813, went from Kingston to Amherstburg on Lake Erie, to command the forces and building programme and to stand in a similar relation under Yeo as Perry did under Chauncey.

On May 25, reinforcements having arrived for the defence of Sackets Harbor, Chauncey followed his squadron to Niagara, from which the Americans were even then bombarding Fort George on the Canadian side in preparation for an attack. Chauncey reported:

> On the 26th, I reconnoitered the Position for landing the Troops and at Night Sounded the Shore and place Buoys to point out the Stations for the Small Vessels. . . . At 3 in the morning the Signal was made for the Fleet to weigh and the Troops were all embarked on board the vessels before 4 . . . it being however nearly

calm the Schooners were obliged to Sweep their Positions. Mr. Trant in the *Julia* and Mr. Mix in the *Growler*, I directed to take a position in the Mouth of the River and Silence a battery near the Light House which from its position commanded the Shore where our Troops were to land. Mr. Stevens in the *Ontario* was directed to take a position to the North of the Light House, so near in fact as to infiltrate the battery and cross the Fire of the *Julia* and *Growler*. Lieut. Pettigrew in the *Conquest* was directed to anchor to the S.E. of the Same battery so near as to open it in the Rear, and Cross the Fire of the *Governor Tompkins*. Lieut. Macpherson in the *Hamilton*, Lieut. Smith in the *Asp*, and Mr. Osgood in the *Scourge* were directed to anchor close to the shore and cover the landing of the Troops.

Perry was present at Chauncey's request to command the seamen and marines landing from the fleet. In a letter, perhaps to his parents, he gave this account:

The ship [*Madison*] was under way, with a light breeze from the eastward, quite fair for us; a thick mist hanging over Newark [sic] and Fort George, the sun breaking forth in the east, the vessels all under way, the lake covered with several hundred large boats, filled with soldiers, horses, and artillery, advancing towards the enemy, altogether formed one of the grandest spectacles I have ever beheld. The breeze now freshened a little, which soon brought us opposite the town of Newark [sic]. The landing place fixed upon was about two miles from the town, up the Niagara. The commodore, observing some of the schooners taking a wrong position, requested me to go in shore and direct them where to anchor.

Perry did this from a small boat, "within musket-shot," and directed *Asp* and *Ontario* to places where they could "enfilade two forts." After making other adjustments: "Observing the schooners did not fire briskly, from the apprehension of injuring our own troops, I went on board the *Hamilton*, of nine guns, commanded by Lieutenant Macpherson, and opened a tremendous fire of grape and canister . . . the enemy could not stand the united effect of the grape and canister from the schooner, and of a well-directed fire from the troops, but broke and fled in great confusion, we plying them with round shot."

According to Myers's account:

The army got into the bateaux, formed in two divisions, and commenced pulling towards the mouth of the Niagara. The morning was foggy, with a light wind, and the vessels getting under way kept company with the boats, a little outside them. The schooners were closest in, and some of them opened on Fort George, while others kept along the coast, scouring the shore with grape and canister as they moved ahead. The *Scourge* came to anchor a short distance above the place selected for the landing, and sprung her broadside to the shore. We now kept up a steady fire with grape and canister,

"The Capture of Fort George, May 27, 1813." *Madison* lies in the foreground, with *Oneida* to her right. On the eastern bank of the Niagara River is Fort Niagara; on the western bank, Fort George.

until the boats had got in-shore and were engaged with the enemy, when we threw round-shot over the heads of our own men upon the English.

Chauncey reported:

Our Troops then advanced in their Brigades. . . . The Enemy who had been concealed in a ravine now advanced in great force to the edge of the Bank to charge our Troops. The Schooners opened so well-directed and tremendous fire of grape and Canister that the Enemy soon retreated from the Bank. Our Troops formed as soon as they landed and immediately ascended the Bank and charged and routed the Enemy in every Action, the Schooners keeping up a constant and well-directed fire upon him in his retreat toward Town.

Myers related,

We had no one hurt, though we were hulled over once or twice. A little rigging was cut . . .
    Just after we had anchored, Mr Bogardus was sent aloft to ascertain if any enemy were to be seen. At first he found nobody; but, after a little while, he called out to have my gun fired at a little thicket of brushwood that lay on an inclined plain, near the water. Mr. Osgood came and elevated the gun and I touched it off. We had been looking out for the blink of muskets, which was one certain guide to find a soldier; and the moment we sent this grist of grape and canister into those bushes, the place lighted up as if a thousand muskets were there. We then gave the chaps the remainder of our broadside. We peppered that wood well, and did a good deal of harm to the troops stationed at the place.

Now the weather changed for the worse: "The Wind had increased so much and hove such a Sea on Shore that the situation of the Fleet had become dangerous and critical," reported

"This grist of grape..." Grapeshot (which looks here exactly like white grapes) was packaged in flannel and tied with string in a criss-cross pattern so as to form a cylindrical package — a flannel shotgun shell. Notice the sword and the huge oars or "sweeps." This group of objects lies on *Hamilton*'s port side beneath the after chain plates.

Chauncey. "I, therefore, made the signal for the Fleet to Weigh and ordered them into the River, where they anchored immediately after the Enemy had abandoned Fort George. The Town and Fort were in quiet possession of our troops at 12 o'clock and the Enemy retreated in the direction toward Queenston."

On the Canadian side, an eye-witness reported: "The contest soon became unequal, more from the destructive fire from his craft than from his troops. Confident I am that any number of his troops would have been successfully repelled, unaided by such an enormous aid of ordnance."

The number of American troops was approximately twenty-three hundred, but soon increased to six thousand; there were less than six hundred British regulars bravely defending the Canadian side. After taking great losses, these retreated towards Queenston, and subsequently westward along the Niagara Peninsula; the Americans did not pursue their advantage.

Hamilton's Lieutenant Macpherson was commended: "He rendered a very important Service in covering the Troops so completely that their loss was trifling."

The return of the American squadron to Sackets Harbor was delayed while Lieutenant Macpherson in *Hamilton* ferried Perry and fifty-five seamen to Lewiston, and received from the upper lake some powder and grapeshot for his squadron.

When Chauncey returned to Sackets Harbor on May 29, he discovered that twelve hundred British troops had landed and attacked the naval base. *Pike*'s stores and the property brought from New York had been fired by an American naval officer acting under orders. *Pike* herself had been set alight, but the conflagration had been extinguished.

"We now kept up a steady fire with canister." Canister consisted of small shot packed into a metal cylinder which was then plugged at the ends with wood, and fired from a cannon or carronade. This canister, with a group of dead-eyes — a form of block pierced with three holes and used to secure the standing rigging — and a dirk, or short sword, lies on *Hamilton*'s port side, just above her main chain plates.

However, the naval base was still intact, and a British opportunity had been lost. Wingfield blamed the failure on the slow timing of that cautious commander, Sir George Prevost. The British squadron, which now consisted of *Moira*, *Beresford* (ex-*Prince Regent*), *Sir Sidney Smith* (ex-*Simcoe*), *Royal George*, and the new *Wolfe*, had been used (supported by approximately forty bateaux) to transport the troops, and Yeo was frustrated at the delay, which cost the British the great advantage of surprise. By Wingfield's account:

> The ships were ready for Sea by the latter part of May, and a strong body of men was assembled at Kingston to make an attack upon the enemy's works at Sackets Harbor, which, if once in our possession, would have put an end to the naval war on Lake Ontario . . . as the Americans had no other harbour along the coast fit for a naval depot.
> At daybreak a light breeze sprang up and we got under way, the boats occasionally laying on their oars to keep company . . . about noon on rounding a point we came in full view of the enemy about ten miles distant, who, immediately they perceived us, commenced firing alarm guns to call in the surrounding militia . . . we received orders to prepare for disembarking the troops, the ships cleared for action . . . about 6 p.m. a fresh breeze sprung up dead on the land, the ships bore up and took in their small sail . . . every heart now beat high with eagerness and expectation, but when nearly within gun-shot of the shores the ships suddenly hauled their wind and stood out to sea, making a signal for the boats to follow. . . .

The order to withdraw had come from Prevost, and this decision caused

> some altercation between the two Commanders — Sir James urging the expediency of an immediate attack, and the Governor alleging

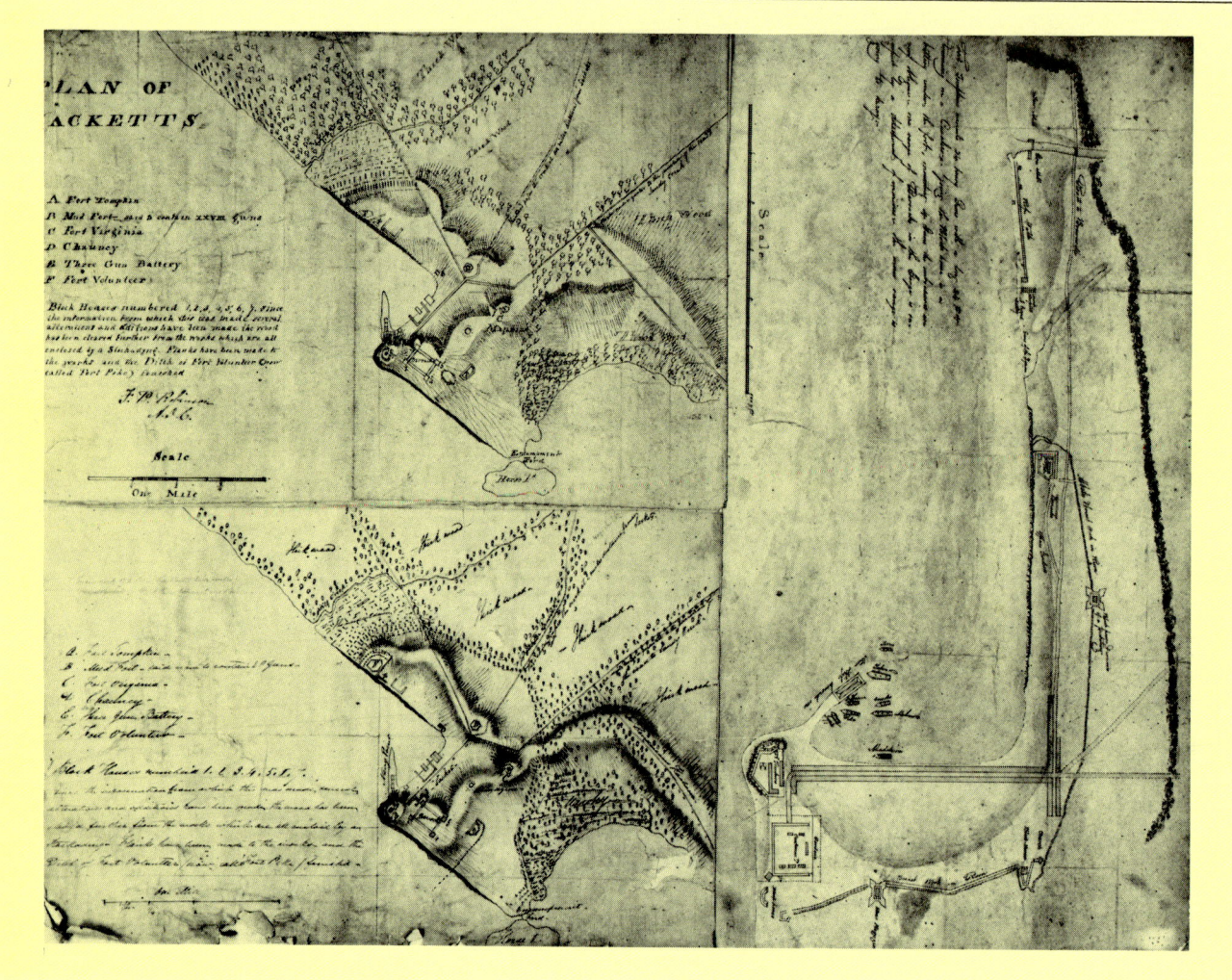

Plans of the fortifications at Sackets Harbor, by a British officer made in 1814.

the decline of the day to defer it; the delay, however, put a great damp upon our spirits, as we plainly saw by our glasses several boats well manned, enter the harbour to reinforce the garrison and well knew they would be receiving reinforcements all the night, as they kept up an incessant firing of minute guns; whereas if we had made a bold dash at once, it is most probable that the troops would have been landed immediately under their batteries, and in the town, under cover of the shipping.

When the British were first sighted, troops defending Sackets were "not above 300 strong," but by the next day American reinforcements had arrived, and the favourable wind had died. The British attack was finally made in disadvantageous circumstances, and eventually a retreat was ordered although "who gave the orders no one knew, the governor and his staff positively denying having done so."

Wingfield states that "we lost nearly 400 men killed and wounded in this disgraceful affair . . . this failure caused a coolness between the Governor and Commodore." After the fact,

Sackets Harbor, 1814. A hamlet before the War of 1812, the community experienced enormous growth as America's naval and military headquarters on the Great Lakes.

the importance of the attack was diminished by Prevost, who described it as a "diversion."

Chauncey reported to Jones: "The regular troops stationed here behaved uncommonly well, they disputed every inch of ground with the Enemy . . ."

Now that Yeo was present on the lake with his experienced seamen and officers and his new ship *Wolfe*, the naval balance of power had shifted. Chauncey felt at a disadvantage, and until *Pike* was "out" on July 20, the British were masters of Lake Ontario.

During this time of control and supremacy, Yeo maintained British communications while he disrupted those of the Americans, "constantly hovering" on the coast; on June 3, he sailed "to co-operate with our army at the head of the lake and annoy the enemy by intercepting all supplies going to his army, and thereby oblige his squadron to come out for its protection."

The Battle of Stoney Creek, fought on June 6, was a Canadian victory and was a turning point in the successful defence of Upper Canada. The Americans retreated eastwards along the Niagara Peninsula to Forty Mile Creek, where Yeo discovered them at daylight on June 8:

> It being calm, the large vessels could not get in, but the *Beresford*, Captain Spilsbury, the *Sir Sidney Smith*, Lieut. Anthony (first of this ship) succeeded in getting close under the enemy's batteries, and by a sharp and well-directed fire soon obliged him to make a precipitate retreat, leaving all his camp equipage, provisions, stores,

etc. behind, which fell into our hands. The *Beresford* also captured all his bateaux laden with stores, etc. Our troops immediately occupied the post, I then proceeded along shore to the westward of the enemy's camp, leaving our army in his front. On the 13th we captured two schooners and some boats going to the enemy with supplies. By them I received information that there was a depot of provisions at Genesee River. I accordingly proceeded off that river, landed some seamen and brought off all the provisions found in the government stores, and also a sloop laden with grain for the army. On the 19th I anchored off the Great Sodus, landed a party of the 1st Regiment of Royal Scots and took off six hundred barrels of flour and pork which had arrived there for their army.

While at Sodus, midway between the Genesee River and Oswego, the British burned the public storehouses, five dwellings, and a hotel; subsequently, Yeo harassed transit between Oswego and Sackets Harbor, and on June 20 he feinted attack on the former.

Thus the British commandant kept the Americans on the defensive: "If the schooners *Lark* and *Fly* are not now at Sackets," Woolsey worriedly wrote to Chauncey during the third week in June, "they must have been taken yesterday by the British boats. They were loaded with powder, shot, and hospital stores for the army." He felt that he could not risk sending the cordage, powder, guns, or cables, which he had on hand, at that time.

On July 1, Yeo threatened a surprise attack on Sackets Harbor; he withdrew because of betrayal by an informer. On July 16, he reported:

> I have used every device in my power to induce the enemy's squadron to come out before his new ship was ready, but to no effect. I am sorry to say she is now manned, and will be ready for sea in a few days.
> Our new brig *Melville* will be launched this week, when the two squadrons will be in as great a force as they can be this year, and immediately we are both ready a general action must take place, as every military operation or success depends entirely on whoever can maintain the naval superiority on this lake.

Yeo, like Chauncey, was, however, reluctant to risk engagement without clear advantage, because to lose was to lose all, although his correspondence makes frequent reference to a desire to engage. Advantage to Yeo, with his carronades, was in rough weather at close quarters; Chauncey's long guns made his squadron superior in calm weather at long range. Neither wished to engage without the "weather gauge"; that is, the upwind position in relation to the other squadron.

One can conjecture that Chauncey spent part of his seven weeks at Sackets Harbor catching up on paperwork. A document dated June 15 and entitled "A Return of Vessels of War belonging to the United States upon Lake Ontario exhibiting their force in Guns and Men" gives statistics relating to *Hamilton* and *Scourge*.

Hamilton, at seventy-six tons, is middle-sized in Chauncey's group of ten schooners, smaller than *Governor Tompkins*, formerly Bronson's *Charles and Ann* at ninety-six tons, or *Fair American* (eighty-two tons), but far larger than *Scourge*, which, listed at forty-five tons, is the smallest member of Chauncey's squadron. *Hamilton* is now listed with nine guns — eight eighteen-pounder carronades and one long twelve-pounder. *Scourge* has eight guns: four long six-pounders and four long four-pounders.

According to this document, *Hamilton* was commanded by a lieutenant commander, who had a crew of fifty-two men, including thirty-three ordinary seamen and nine marines; *Scourge* carried thirty-three men, among them a marine and twenty-six ordinary seamen; she was commanded by a sailing-master. However, perhaps the best record of crew members are the muster rolls from this period, which show the ship's complements as they were when the schooners left on their last voyage.

We can note from *Hamilton*'s muster roll that Lieutenant Macpherson was transferred to *Pike* on July 13, and Lieutenant Walter Winter replaced him in the command of the schooner.

Pike was ready on July 20 and Chauncey was out on the lake with his squadron on July 21. He sailed first to Niagara, where he embarked troops; an attack on Burlington Heights was considered but it was decided the defence was too strong. From thence, the squadron proceeded to York on the thirtieth. Here troops landed with no opposition, destroyed eleven boats, captured provisions, cannon, shot, and powder, and burned barracks and public storehouses in retaliation for British incendiary action at Great Sodus.

Chauncey returned to Niagara on August 3; Yeo had left Kingston on August 2, and at dawn on Saturday, August 7, Yeo found the American squadron at anchor.

PART THREE

Shipwreck

Wind during the night from the westward and after midnight squally. Kept all hands at quarters and beat to windward in hopes to gain the wind of the enemy. At 2 a.m. missed two of our schooners. At daylight discovered the missing schooners to be the Hamilton *and* Scourge. *Soon after spoke to Governor Tompkins who informed me that the* Hamilton *and* Scourge *both overset and sunk in a heavy squall about two o'clock, and, distressing to relate, every soul perished except sixteen [sic]. This fatal accident deprived me at once of the services of two valuable officers, Lieutenant Winter and Sailing-Master Osgood, and two of my best schooners, mounting together nineteen guns.*

COMMODORE CHAUNCEY
to the Secretary of
the United States Navy

ON SATURDAY, AUGUST 7, 1813, AT FIRST DAYLIGHT, CHAUNCEY discovered Yeo's fleet bearing down upon him as he lay at anchor off Niagara.

It was a fine summer's day, and in expectation of viewing the long-awaited naval battle on the lake, crowds of spectators gathered on the shore and the overlooking heights.

Yeo reported to Prevost:

We arrived off Niagara Saturday morning having had nothing but calm and light airs, all the way from Kingston. The Enemy's squadron was at anchor but got under way immediately on seeing us — stood out, and shew'd every disposition to engage, but on coming within four miles of us, he fired his broadside (which did not reach halfway). Wore round and stood close in with Niagara.

In Chauncey's words:

On the 7th at daylight the enemy's fleet consisting of two ships, two brigs and two large schooners were discovered bearing W.N.W., distant about five or six miles, wind at west. At 5 weighed with the fleet and manoeuvred to gain the wind. At 9, having passed to lee-ward of the enemy's line and abreast of his van ship, the *Wolfe*, hoisted our colours and fired a few guns to ascertain whether we could reach him with our shot. Finding they fell short I wore and hauled upon a wind on the starboard tack, the rear of our schooners then about six miles astern.

"We got two small brass guns at York, four-pounders, I believe, which Mr. Osgood clapped into our two spare ports forward. This gave us ten guns in all, sixes and fours." *Scourge*'s forward-most port gun. Note the thole pin (used to support a sweep when rowing) set into the bottom of the gunport.

"Catch a turn... around the *pommelions* of the guns." The securing rope still remains around the pommelion of this port cannon on *Scourge*. Note the wedge used to adjust the elevation of the gun.

Myers relates:

While we were in the river, Sir James Yeo hove in sight with two ships, two brigs, and two schooners. We had thirteen sail in all, such as they were, and immediately got under way, and manoeuvred for the weather-gauge. All the enemy's vessels had regular quarters, and the ships were stout craft. Our squadron sailed very unequally, some being pretty fast, and others as dull as droggers. Nor were we more than half fitted out. On board the *Scourge* the only square-sail we had was made out of an English marquee we had laid our hands on at York, the first time we were there. I ought to say too, that we got two small brass guns at York, four-pounders, I believe, which Mr. Osgood clapped into our two spare ports forward. This gave us ten guns in all, sixes and fours.

Chauncey tells us:

The enemy wore in succession, and hauled upon a wind on the same tack, but finding that we should be able to weather him upon the next tack, he tacked and made all sail northward. As soon as our rear vessels could fetch his wake, tacked and made all sail in chase. In the afternoon the wind became very light and towards night quite calm. The schooners used their sweeps all the afternoon in order to close with the enemy, but without success. Late in the afternoon I made the signal of recall and formed in close order.

It was a calm August evening, and there was no sense of foreboding, no forewarning of a treacherous change in the weather. Myers relates:

> It was a lovely evening, not a cloud visible, and the lake being as smooth as a looking-glass. The English fleet was but a short distance to the northward of us; so near, indeed, that we could almost count their ports. They were becalmed, like ourselves, and a little scattered.
>
> Towards evening, all light craft were doing the same, to close with the Commodore. Our object was to get together, lest the enemy should cut off some of our small vessels during the night . . .
>
> A little before sunset, Mr. Osgood [the captain] ordered us to pull in our sweeps . . . we took [them] in as ordered, laying them athwart the deck, in readiness to be used when wanted. The vessels ahead and stern of us were, generally, within speaking distance. Just as the sun went below the horizon, George Turnblatt, a Swede, who was our gunner, came to me, and said he thought we ought to secure our guns, for we had been cleared for action all day, and the crew at quarters. We were still at quarters, in name, but the petty officers were allowed to move about, and as much license was given to the people as was wanted. I answered that I would gladly secure mine if he would get an order for it; but as we were still at quarters, and there lay John Bull, we might get a slap at him in the night. On this the gunner said he would go aft and speak to Mr. Osgood on the subject. He did so, but met the captain (as we always called Mr. Osgood) at the break of the quarter-deck. When George had told his errand, the captain looked at the heavens, and remarked that the night was so calm there could be no great use in securing the guns, and the English were so near we should certainly engage, if there came a breeze; that the men would sleep at their quarters, of course, and would be ready to take care of their guns, but that he might catch a turn with the side-tackle-falls around the pommelions of the guns, which would be sufficient. He then ordered the boatswain to call all hands aft, to the break of the quarter-deck.
>
> As soon as the people had collected, Mr. Osgood said: "You must be pretty well fagged out, men; I think we may have a hard night's work yet, and I wish you to get your suppers, and then catch as much sleep as you can, at your guns." He then ordered the purser's steward to splice the main-brace. These were the last words I ever heard from Mr. Osgood. As soon as he gave the order he went below . . .
>
> The schooner, at this time, was under her mainsail, jib, and fore-topsail. The foresail was brailed, and the foot stopped, and the flying-jib was stowed. None of the halyards were racked, nor sheets stoppered. This was a precaution we always took, on account of the craft's being so tender.
>
> We first spliced the main-brace, and then got our suppers, eating between the guns, where we generally messed, indeed. One of my messmates, Tom Goldsmith, was captain of the gun next to me, and as we sat there finishing our suppers, I says to him, "Tom, bring up that rug that you pinned at Little York, and that will do for both of us to stow ourselves away under." Tom went down and got

"All the time I kept shouting to the man at the wheel to put the helm hard down." Myers seems to have been speaking figuratively; all evidence points to the fact that *Scourge* had a tiller rather than a wheel. The rudder post, with its evident fitting for a tiller, is in the foreground above. Behind is the block at the vessel's stern into which the mainsail sheet ran.

Hamilton's tiller, by which the ship was steered. Steering the ship would have required considerable strength in a stiff breeze.

the rug, which was an article for the camp that he had laid hands on, and it made us a capital bed-quilt. As all hands were pretty well tired, we lay down, with our heads on shot-boxes, and soon went to sleep.

In speaking of the canvas that was set, I ought to have said something of the state of our decks. The guns had the side-tackles fastened as I have mentioned. There was a box of canister, and another of grape, at each gun, besides extra stands of both, under the shot-racks. There was also one grummet of round-shot at every gun, besides the racks being filled. Each gun's crew slept at the gun and its opposite, thus dividing the people pretty equally on both sides of the deck. Those who were stationed below, slept below. I think it probable that, as the night grew cool, as it always does on fresh waters, some of the men stole below to get warmer berths. This was easily done in that craft, as we had but two regular officers on board, the acting boatswain and gunner being little more than two of ourselves.

I was soon asleep, as sound as if lying in the bed of a king. How long my nap lasted, or what took place in the interval, I cannot say. I awoke, however, in consequence of large drops of rain falling on my face. Tom Goldsmith awoke at the same moment. When I opened my eyes, it was so dark I could not see the length of the deck. I arose and spoke to Tom, telling him it was about to rain, and that I meant to do down and get a nip, out of a little stuff we kept in our mess-chest, and I would bring up the bottle if he wanted a taste. Tom answered, "This is nothing; we're neither pepper nor salt." One of the black men spoke, and asked me to bring up the bottle, and give him a nip too. All this took half a minute, perhaps. I now remember to have heard a strange rushing noise to windward as I went towards the forward hatch, though it made no impression on me at the time. We had been lying between the starboard guns, which was the weather side of the vessel, if there were any weather side to it, there not being a breath of air, and no motion to the water, and I passed round to the

"The hatch was so small that two men could not pass at a time, and I felt my way to it in no haste. One hand was on the bitts (foreground) and a foot was on the ladder when a flash of lightning almost blinded me." Note the small object on the deck to the left of the mast: this is probably the schooner's chimney.

larboard side in order to find the ladder which led up in that direction. The hatch was so small that two men could not pass at a time, and I felt my way to it, in no haste. One hand was on the bitts, and a foot was on the ladder, when a flash of lightning almost blinded me. The thunder came at the next instant, and with it a rushing of winds that fairly smothered the clap.

The instant I was aware there was a squall, I sprang for the jib-sheet. Being captain of the forecastle, I knew where to find it, and threw it loose at a jerk. In doing this, I jumped on a man named Leonard Lewis, and called on him to lend me a hand. I next let fly the larboard, or lee top-sail-sheet, got hold of the clew-line, and, assisted by Lewis, got the clew half up. All this time I kept shouting to the man at the wheel to put his helm "hard down." The water was now up to my breast, and I knew the schooner must go over. Lewis had not said a word, but I called out to him to shift for himself, and belaying the clew-line, in hauling myself forward of the foremast, I received a blow from the jib-sheet that came near to breaking my arm....

All this occupied less than a minute. The flashes of lightning were incessant, and nearly blinded me. Our decks seemed on fire, and yet I could see nothing. I heard no hail, no order, no call; but the schooner was filled with the shrieks and cries of the men to leeward, who were lying jammed under the guns, shot-boxes, shot, and other heavy things that had gone down as the vessel fell over. The starboard second gun, from forward, had capsized, and come down directly over the hatch, and I caught a glimpse of a man struggling to get past it. Apprehension of this gun had induced me to drag myself forward of the mast where I received the blow mentioned.

I succeeded in hauling myself up to windward, and in getting into the schooner's fore-channels. Here I met William Deer, the boatswain, and a black boy of the name of Philips, who was the powder-boy of our gun. "Deer, she's gone!" I said. The boatswain made no answer, but walked out on the forerigging, towards the head-mast. He probably had some vague notion that the schooner's masts would be out of the water if she went down, and took this course as the safest. The boy was in the chains the last I saw of him.

I now crawled aft, on the upper side of the bulwarks, amid a most awful and infernal din of thunder, and shrieks, and dazzling flashes of lightning; the wind blowing all the while like a tornado. When I reached the port of my own gun, I put a foot in, thinking to step on the muzzle of the piece; but it had gone to leeward with all the rest, and I fell through the port, until I brought up with my arms. I struggled up again, and continued working my way aft. As I got abreast of the main-mast, I saw someone had let run the halyards. I soon reached the beckets of the sweeps, and found four in them. I could not swim a stroke, and it crossed my mind to get one of the sweeps to keep me afloat. In striving to jerk the becket clear, it parted, and the foreward ends of the four sweeps rolled down the schooner's side into the water. This caused the other ends to slide, and all the sweeps got away from me. I then crawled quite aft, as far as the fashion-piece. The water was pouring down the cabin companion-way like a sluice, and as I stood for an instant on the fashion-piece, I saw Mr. Osgood, with his head and part of his shoulders through one of the cabin windows, struggling to get out. He must have been within six feet of me. I saw him but a moment, by means of a flash of lightning, and I think he must have seen me. At the same time, there was a man visible at the end of the main-boom, holding on to the clew of the sail. I do not know who it was. The man probably saw me, and that I was about to spring, for he called out, "Don't jump overboard! — don't jump overboard! The schooner is righting."

I was not in a state of mind to reflect much on anything. I do not think more than three or four minutes, if as many, had passed since the squall struck us, and there I was standing on the vessel's quarter, led by Providence more than by any discretion of my own. It now came across me that if the schooner should right she was filled, and must go down, and that she might carry me with her in the suction. I made a spring, therefore, and fell into the water several feet from the place where I had stood. It is my opinion the schooner sank as I left her.

I went down some distance myself, and when I came up to the surface, I began to swim vigorously for the first time in my life. I think I swam several yards, but of course will not pretend to be certain of such a thing, at such a moment, until I felt my hand hit something hard. I made another stroke and felt my hand pass down the side of an object that I knew at once to be a clincher-built boat. I belonged to this boat, and now I recollected that she had been towing astern. Until that instant I had not thought of her, but thus was I led in the dark to the best possible means of saving my life. I made a grab at the gunwale, and caught in the stern-sheets. Had I swum another yard, I should have passed the boat, and missed her altogether! I got in without any difficulty, being all alive and much excited.

My first look was for the schooner. She had disappeared, and I supposed she was just settling under water. It rained as if the flood-gates of heaven were opened, and it lighteninged awfully. It did not seem to me that there was a breath of air, and the water was unruffled, the effects of the rain excepted. All this I saw, as it might be, at a glance. But my chief concern was to preserve my own life. I was coxswain of this very boat, and had made it fast to the taffrail that same afternoon, with a round turn and two half-hitches, by its best painter. Of course I expected the vessel would drag the boat down with her, for I had no knife to cut the painter. There was a gang-board in the boat, however, which lay fore and aft, and I thought this might keep me afloat until some of the fleet should pick me up. To clear this gang-board, then, and get into the water, was my first object. I ran forward to throw off the lazy-painter that was coiled on its end, and in doing this, I caught the boat's painter in my hand by accident. A pull satisfied me that it was all clear! Someone on board must have cast off this painter, and then lost the chance of getting into the boat by accident. At all events I was safe, and I now dared to look about me.

My only chance of seeing was during the flashes, and these left me almost blind. I had thrown the gang-board into the water, and I now called out to encourage the men, telling them I was in the boat. I could hear many around me, and occasionally I saw the

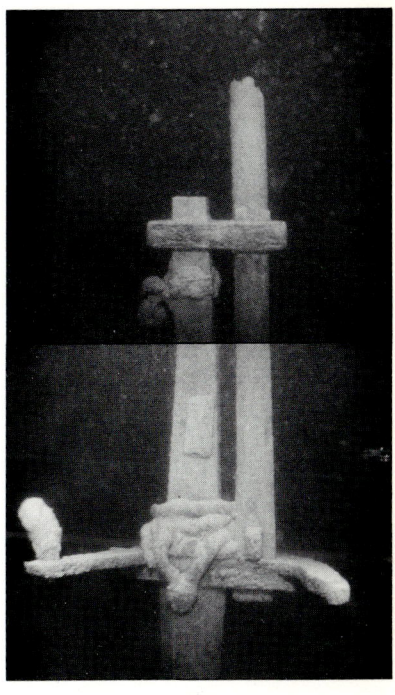

"The boatswain made no answer, but walked out on the fore-rigging, towards the head-mast." The masthead of *Scourge*'s foremast is broken off but the joining of the lower mast to its topmast is still intact.

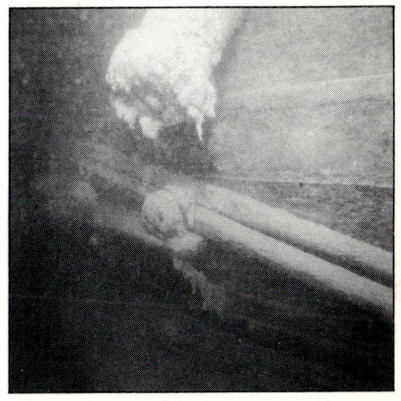

"I soon reached the beckets of the sweeps . . ." Myers released the sweeps secured to the starboard side, but the port sweeps have slipped down to rest along the schooner's main channels.

"As I stood for an instant on the fashion-piece, I saw Mr. Osgood, with his head and part of his shoulders through one of the cabin windows, struggling to get out."

heads of men struggling in the lake. There being no proper place to scull in, I got an oar in the after rowlock and made out to scull a little in that fashion. I now saw a man quite near the boat, and, hauling in the oar, made a spring amidships, catching this poor fellow by the collar. He was very near gone, and I had a great deal of difficulty in getting him in over the gunwale. Our joint weight brought the boat down, so low that she shipped a good deal of water. This turned out to be Leonard Lewis, the young man who had helped me to clew up the fore-topsail. He could not stand, and spoke with difficulty. I asked him to crawl aft, out of the water, which he did, lying down in the stern-sheets.

I now looked about me and heard another; leaning over the gunwale, I got a glimpse of a man, struggling, quite near the boat, I caught him by the collar too, and had to drag him in very much in the way I had done with Lewis. This proved to be Lemuel Bryant, the man who had been wounded by a hot shot, at York,

Myers rescued himself and his shipmates in *Scourge*'s ship's boat, but *Hamilton*'s boat lies astern the schooner. Carvel-built (smooth-sided) as opposed to Scourge's boat which Myers describes as clinker-built (overlapping strakes), she is intended to be either rowed or sailed (the hole in the thwart — or seat — was designed to support a mast).

while the commodore was on board us. His wound had not yet healed, but he was less exhausted than Lewis. He could not help me, however, lying down in the bottom of the boat, the instant he was able.

For a few moments I now heard no more in the water, and I began to scull again. By my calculation I moved a few yards, and must have got over the spot where the schooner went down. Here, in the flashes, I saw many heads, the men swimming in confusion and at random. By this time little was said, the whole scene being one of fearful struggle and frightful silence. It still rained, but the flashes were less frequent and less fierce. They told me, afterwards, in the squadron, that it thundered awfully, but I cannot say I heard a clap after I struck the water. The next man caught the boat himself. It was a mulatto, from Martinique, who was Mr. Osgood's steward, and I helped him in. He was much exhausted, though an excellent swimmer, but alarm nearly deprived him of his strength. He kept saying, "Oh! Masser Ned — Oh! Masser Ned!" and lay down in the bottom of the boat like the two others, I taking care to shove him over to the larboard side, so as to trim our small craft.

I kept calling out to encourage the swimmers, and presently I heard a voice saying, "Ned, I'm here, close by you." This was Tom Goldsmith, a messmate, and the very man under whose rug I had been sleeping at quarters. He did not want much help, getting in, pretty much, by himself. I asked him if he were able to help me. "Yes, Ned," he answered, "I'll stand by you to the last; what shall I do?" I told him to take his tarpaulin and to bail the boat, which, by this time, was a third full of water. This he did, while I sculled a little ahead. "Ned," says Tom, "she's gone down with her colours flying, for her pennant came near getting a round turn around my body, and carrying me down with her. Davy has made a good haul, and he gave us a close shave, but he didn't get you and me." In this manner did this thoughtless sailor express himself, as soon as rescued from the grasp of death! Seeing something on the water, I asked Tom to take my oar, while I sprang to the gunwale and caught Mr. Bogardus, the master's mate, who was clinging to one of the sweeps. I hauled him in, and he told me he thought someone had hold of the other end of the sweep. It was so dark, however, we could not see even that distance. I hauled the sweep along until I found Ebenezer Duffy, a mulatto, and the ship's cook. He could not swim a stroke, and was nearly gone. I got him in alone, Tom bailing, lest the boat, which was quite small, should swamp with us.

As the boat drifted along, she reached another man, whom I caught also by the collar. I was afraid to haul this person in amidships, the boat being now so deep, and so small, and so I dragged him ahead, and hauled him in over the bows. This man was the pilot, whose name I never knew. He was a lake-man and had been aboard with us the whole summer. The poor fellow was almost gone, and like all the rest, with the exception of Tom, he lay down and said not a word.

We had now as many in the boat as it would carry, and Tom and myself thought it would not do to take in any more. It is true we saw no more, everything around us appearing still as death, the pattering of the rain excepted. Tom began to bail again, and I commenced hallooing. I sculled about several minutes thinking of giving others a tow, or of even hauling in one or two more, after we got the water out of the boat; but we found no one else. I think it probable I sculled away from the spot, as there was nothing to guide me. I suppose, however, that by this time all the Scourges had gone down, for no more were ever heard from.

Tom Goldsmith and myself now put our heads together as to what best to be done. We were both afraid of falling into the enemy's hands, for they might have bore up in the squall and run down near us. On the whole, however, we thought the distance between the two squadrons was too great for this; at all events, something must be done at once. So we began to row, in what direction even we did not know. It still rained as hard as it could pour, though there was not a breath of wind. The lightning came now at considerable intervals, and the gust was evidently passing away towards the broader parts of the lake. While we were rowing and talking about our chance of falling in with the enemy, Tom cried out to me to "avast pulling." He had seen a vessel by a flash, and he thought she was English, from her size. As he said she was a schooner, however, I thought it must be one of our own craft, and got her direction from him. At the next flash, I saw her, and felt satisfied she belonged to us. Before we began to pull, however, we were hailed. "Boat ahoy!" I answered. "If you pull another stroke, I'll fire into you," came back. "What boat's that? Lay on your oars or I'll fire into you." It was clear we were mistaken ourselves for an enemy, and I called out to know what schooner it was. No answer was given, though the threat to fire was repeated, if we pulled another stroke. I now turned to Tom and said, "I know that voice — that is old Trant." Tom thought we were "in the wrong shop." I now sang out, "This is the *Scourge*'s boat; our schooner is gone down, and we want to come alongside." A voice now called from the schooner — "Is that you, Ned?" This I knew was my old shipmate and schoolfellow, Jack Mallet, who was acting as boatswain on the *Julia*, the schooner commanded by Sailing-Master James Trant, one of the oddities of the service, and a man with whom the blow often came as soon as the word. I had known Mr. Trant's voice, and felt more afraid he would fire into us than I had done of anything which had occurred that fearful night. Mr. Trant himself now called out, "Oh-ho; give way, boys, and come alongside." This we did, and a very few strokes took us up to the *Julia*, where we were received with the utmost kindness. The men were passed out of the boat, while I gave Mr. Trant an account of all that had happened. This took but a minute or two.

Mr. Trant now enquired in what direction the *Scourge* had gone down, and as soon as I told him, in the best manner I could, he called out to Jack Mallet: "Oh-ho, Mallet — take four hands, and go in the boat and see what you can do — take a lantern, and I will show a light on the water's edge, so you may know me." Mallet did as ordered, and was off in less than three minutes after we got alongside. . . .

Mr. Trant now called the Scourges aft, and asked more of the particulars. He then gave us a glass of grog all round, and made his own crew splice the main-brace. The Julias now offered us dry clothes. I got a change from Jack Reilly, who had been an old messmate, and with whom I had always been on good terms. It knocked off raining, but we shifted ourselves at the galley fire below. I then went on deck and presently we hear the boat pulling back. It soon came alongside, bringing in it four more men that had been found floating about on sweeps and gratings. On inquiry, it turned out that these men belonged to the *Hamilton*, [commanded by] Lieutenant Winter — a schooner that had gone down in the same squall that carried us over. These men were very much exhausted, too, and we all went below and were told to turn in.

I had been so much excited during the scenes through which I had just passed, and had been so much stimulated by grog that, as yet, I had not felt much of the depression natural to such events. I even slept soundly that night, nor did I turn out until six the next morning.

When I got on deck, there was a fine breeze; it was a lovely day, and the lake was perfectly smooth. Our fleet was in a good line, in pretty close order, with the exception of the *Governor Tompkins* [commanded by] Lieutenant Tom Brown, which was a little to leeward, but carrying a press of sail to close with the commodore. Mr. Trant, perceiving that the *Tompkins* wished to speak to us in passing, brailed his foresail and let her luff up close under our lee. "Two of the schooners, the *Hamilton* and the *Scourge*, have gone down in the night," called out Mr. Brown, "for I have picked up four of the *Hamilton*'s." "Oh-ho!" answered Mr. Trant, "that's no news at all, for I have picked up twelve; eight of the *Scourge*'s and four of the *Hamilton*'s — aft fore-sheet."

These were all that were ever saved from the two schooners, which must have had near a hundred souls on board them. The two commanders, Lieutenant Winter and Mr. Osgood, were both lost, and with Mr. Winter went down, I believe, one or two young gentlemen. The squadron could not have moved much between the time when the accidents happened and that when I came on deck, or we must have come round and gone over the same ground again, for we now passed many relics of the scene, floating about in the water. I saw sponges, gratings, sweeps, hats, etc., scattered about, and in passing ahead we saw one of the last that we tried to catch; Mr. Trant ordering it done, as he said it must have been Lieutenant Winter's. We did not succeed, however, nor was any article taken on board. A good look-out was kept for men from aloft, but none were seen from any of the vessels. The lake had swallowed up the rest of the two crews, and the *Scourge*, as had been often predicted, had literally become a coffin to a large portion of her people.

The British do not seem to have immediately noted the loss of *Hamilton* and *Scourge*. *Wolfe*'s log for Sunday morning states: "Light breezes variable, very warm weather. At 5: The 40 Mile Creek bore SSW distance about 8 miles, wind southerly. Saw the Enemy squadron bearing E & by S about four or five leagues standing to the westward on the larboard tack. At ditto made sail and stood towards him."

Even the next morning, Yeo had not received intelligence of the sinking. At 11 a.m., off York, he reported to Prevost: "On

"The lake had swallowed up the rest of the two crews." Fifty-three men died in the combined capsizing of *Hamilton* and *Scourge*; there were only nineteen survivors. This was the largest single loss of life on the lakes during the War of 1812.

Sunday it was calm, when he sent all his schooners, to sweep after us — but about two o'clock a breeze springing up, we stood for them and it was with some difficulty he gained the anchorage off the river where he remained all night."

Chauncey assumed that Yeo knew of his loss:

> This accident giving to the enemy decidedly the superiority, I thought he would take the advantage of it, particularly as by a change of wind he was again brought dead to the windward of me. Formed, the wind upon the larboard tack, and hove to. Soon after 6 a.m. the enemy bore up and set studding sails, apparently with an intention to bring us to action. When he had approached us within about four miles, he brought to on the starboard tack. Finding that the enemy had no intention of bringing us to action, I edged away to gain the land in order to have the advantage of the land breeze in the afternoon. It soon after fell calm and I directed the schooners to sweep up and engage the enemy. About noon we got a light breeze from the eastward; I took *Oneida* in tow, as she sails badly, and stood for the enemy. When the van of our schooners was within one-and-a-half or two miles of his rear, the wind shifted to the westward, which again brought him to windward. As soon

Muster rolls of *Hamilton* and *Scourge* from July 1 until August 8, 1813. Initials in the ninth column stand for *Discharged, Discharged Dead* — and *Prisoner*. The schooner *Julia* which rescued Myers and his shipmates was captured with a second schooner, *Growler*, by Yeo on August 10.

as the breeze struck him he bore up for the schooners in order to cut them off before they could rejoin me, but with their sweeps and the breeze soon reaching them also they were soon in their station. The enemy finding himself foiled in his attempt on the schooners hauled his wind and hove to. It soon after became very squally, and the appearance of its continuing so during the night, and as we had been at quarters for nearly forty-eight hours, and being apprehensive of separating from some of the heavy sailing schooners in the squall induced me to run in towards Niagara and anchor outside the bar.

Monday was spent in more manoeuvring; on Tuesday, Yeo cut out and captured two of Chauncey's schooners, *Julia* and *Growler*. By means of this capture, the British received sure knowledge of the capsizing of *Hamilton* and *Scourge*.

Entry in *Wolfe*'s log, August 8, 1813. Information from this log, combined with Myers's observations, gave an historic record of the location of the two schooners which proved an invaluable aid to searchers in the early 1970s.

The two squadrons on Lake Ontario on August 10, 1813, two days after the capsizing of *Hamilton* and *Scourge*. On this day Yeo captured *Julia* (with Myers aboard) and *Growler*.

Action on Lake Ontario, September 11, 1813. Because of the uneven sailing qualities and armaments of their fleets, both Chauncey and Yeo were fighting "unconventional warfare." In addition, they both had the responsibility of supporting their armies. By contrast, traditional naval battles were then fought by two fleets sailing in two parallel lines, fighting broadside to broadside.

On Wednesday, August 11, Yeo reported to Prevost:

Wolfe, off York, 11th August, 1813
$\frac{1}{2}$ past 1 P.M.

My Dear Sir,

Yesterday evening the enemy's squadron stood for us with a fine breeze from the east. Ours was becalmed off the post at 12 Mile Creek. At sunset a breeze came off the land which gave us the wind of the enemy, and I stood for them, on which he immediately stood from us under as much sail as his schooners could keep up with him. He was in a long line, *Pike*, *Madison*, *Oneida*, six schooners and two to windward to take our vessels as we came up. At 11 we came within gun shot of the schooners, when they opened a brisk fire and from going so fast it was more than an hour before we could pass them. At this time all our squadron was two or three miles astern of the *Wolfe*. On coming up with the *Madison* and *Pike* they put before the wind and made sail, firing their stern chase guns. I found it impossible to get the squadron up with them, as the *Wolfe* was the only ship that could keep up. I therefore made sail between them and the two schooners to windward, while I captured the *Julia* and *Growler*, each mounting one long 32 and one long 12 with a complement of forty men.

I am also happy to acquaint you that two of his largest schooners, the *Hamilton*, of nine guns, and the *Scourge*, of ten guns, upset the night before last in carrying sail to keep from us, and all on board perished, in number about one hundred. This has reduced his squadron to ten and increased ours to eight, but they will take men from the [our] ships.

I feel confident that by watching every proper opportunity we should get the better of him, but as long as he is determined to sacrifice everything to his own safety I shall never in this narrow water be able to bring the two ships to action, as I have no vessel that sails sufficiently well to second me.

This conduct he cannot persevere in long for his own honour, as the loss of all his schooners, (which I must ever have in my power), will be an indelible disgrace, and I am at a loss to know how he will account to his government for it.

The *Pike* mounts 28 long 24-pounders with four hundred and twenty men, the *Madison* twenty-two 32-pounder carronades and three hundred and forty men. (Good head money!) Their squadron took on board the day before yesterday nine boats full of troops, I suppose to repel boarders.

I am happy to add that the *Wolfe* has not received any material damage and no one hurt on board. I am now landing the prisoners and repairing the damages of the *Growler*, who has lost her bowsprit and [is] otherwise much cut up.

It concerns me to find I have such a wary opponent, as it harasses me beyond my strength. I am very unwell and I believe nothing but the nature of the service keeps me up.

I must close this, which is more than I have my eyes for the last forty-eight hours, and hope my next will be more acceptable.

"The loss of the *Growler* and *Julia* in the manner in which they have been lost, is mortifying in the extreme," wrote Chauncey upon his return to Sackets Harbor on August 13, after a bit of stormy weather. He assessed the British squadron: "From what I have been able to discover of the movements of the enemy he has no intention of engaging except he can get decidedly the advantage of wind and weather, and as his vessels in squadron sail better than our squadron he can always avoid an action unless I can gain the wind and have sufficient daylight to bring him to action before dark. His object evidently is to harass us by night attacks . . . ."

Yeo's corresponding assessment given at the same time was:

I much fear Mr. Chauncey will not engage if he can help it, except in his own port or in a calm when his schooners would gain him the Victory without his having a shot fired at him. . . . The *Pike* is a very fine large ship but appears to be very unwieldy, and unmanageable and from the manner she is worked, should judge is not complete with seamen, the *Madison* is about the size of the *Wolfe*, sails well and is managed much better than the *Pike*, the *Oneida* is small and sails bad, and the schooners tho' formidable in a calm are very contemptible otherwise as they have not the least shelter for their men.

My hope is they may remain out at night when we may be able to close with them before they see us, and from their numbers they will be much dispersed.

During the next few weeks, the two squadrons pursued one another around the lake. There was some long-range firing near the Genesee River on September 11; on September 28, after an hour-long exchange of fire west of Toronto Harbour, during which both *Wolfe* and *Pike* were damaged, Yeo withdrew and, pursued westward by Chauncey's squadron, sought shelter under the British batteries at Burlington Heights.

It was generally thought that the channel there, which joined the lake and the sheltered bay beyond, was too shallow for a large ship to pass. But Yeo had on board *Wolfe*, as acting master and pilot, a twenty-two-year-old Canadian, James Richardson, the son of a lake captain, who by a brilliant piece of seamanship, combined with intimate local knowledge, brought the British squadron through the channel in the sand-bar to the safety of the bay. (For his heroic action, Richardson — who became a clergyman in 1818 and, in 1858, a bishop — was awarded an annual pension of £100.)

But, by that time, the entire nature of the conflict in Upper Canada had changed: on September 10, at the southwestern end

The storming of Fort Oswego, May 6, 1814. This British attack destroyed American stores and delayed the equipping of fleet at Sackets Harbor.

of Lake Erie, off Sandusky, Perry had won a brilliant naval victory, and Barclay suffered an honourable defeat.

The results of Perry's victory were far-reaching. Detroit was retaken by the Americans, and this enabled Harrison to pursue the British forces along the north shore of Lake Erie, where he forced battle at the Thames River. Tecumseh was slain, and his Indian peoples demoralized.

After the Battle of Lake Erie, news of which was received with jubilation in the United States, Chauncey shared in the congratulations. During the ensuing year, however, his bustle and efficiency were transformed to lassitude; he fell ill; eventually he exhibited such odd behaviour that President Madison decided to replace him in his command by the naval hero Stephen Decatur. However, the plan was dropped, and Chauncey stayed in command until the end of the war.

Yeo, on the other hand, faced with a numerically superior fleet, took advantage of Chauncey's difficulties and faults and avoided battle unless he was clearly in a superior position. His mission was to keep his fleet intact, to support his army, and deny the American fleet control of Lake Ontario. This was not a heroic policy, but certainly it was a war of nerves (Yeo was observed to smash his telescope on a cannon in frustration after having gazed at Chauncey through it). However, it resulted in the continuation of the see-sawing ship-building race, and it did have the effect of preserving the border. A much publicised British attack on the village and decrepit fort at Oswego in 1814 destroyed some stores and delayed the equipping of the American fleet, but otherwise brought little but publicity to the British, who celebrated the attack with fascinating engravings.

For the rest, on the Niagara Peninsula, the Americans eventually retired across the river December 10, 1813, leaving the town of Niagara in flames. The latter act ended small courtesies — like the attempted return of Mrs. McCormick's trunks, which had

Surprize capturing *Star*: an ocean-scene example of single ship action. Because shot was greatly slowed by water, it was hard to sink a wooden ship. Therefore, opponents battered away at one another until one was disabled and forced to surrender. In single ship action, that is, when two ships fought alone, an excellent tactic was to "rake" one's opponent by sailing across his defenceless bow or stern, and fire the length of his ship. Notice the schooner's "brailed" mainsail out of the way of the fighting seamen.

The launching of *St. Lawrence*, 112 guns, at Kingston, September 10, 1814.

marked the first part of the war — and triggered a retaliatory burning of Buffalo, as the firing on York led to the burning of Washington.

An American attempt on Montreal was too late to be successful; the Royal Navy's blockade of the east coast of the United States was effective; a second effort to take the Niagara Peninsula failed, as did the attempt to re-take Michilimackinac. Although

Kingston Harbour, Lake Ontario — July, 1815. Idle warships were the sign of peace.

the supply ship *Nancy* was burned, the island was defended by a brilliant small-boat action.

After Napoleon's exile in 1814, the British mounted a three-pronged attack on the United States: on Lake Champlain, on the Chesapeake, and at New Orleans. In each case, defence was ultimately successful and significant: Lieutenant Thomas Macdonough achieved a brilliant naval victory on Lake Champlain; the British campaign on the Chesapeake gave the United States the White House and its national anthem, "Star-Spangled Banner"; and the Battle of New Orleans allowed Andrew Jackson to prove his mettle, and thus launch his political career.

The peace conference opened at Ghent, Belgium, in August, 1814. The treaty was signed on December 24, 1814, and ratified early in the new year of 1815. It was a treaty which virtually returned to the territorial *status quo ante*. However, in Canada, the successful and vigorous defence — initiated by Brock's brilliant strategy, and supported by his years of careful preparation of a professional military force — was the catalyst that formed a sense of nationhood, and paved the way for the democratic reforms of the 1840s and the Confederation of 1867. The United States also experienced a development of national spirit, and a new sense of autonomy.

An indication of a fresh spirit of respect and cooperation was the Rush-Bagot convention, signed in 1817, between Britain and the United States; this led to a practical disarmament on the United States-Canadian frontier. In addition, diplomatic sophistication, enormous national growth, and national pride on both sides of the border provided a sustaining milieu for an extraordinary and even bemusing public discussion, lasting for more than one hundred years, concerning the legalities of the capture of *Lord Nelson* and restitution due her owners.

A post-war view of Sackets Harbor.

PART FOUR

Hamilton *and* Scourge *Found*

"Ahh . . . fantastique . . . magnifique . . . ah la la . . . beautiful . . . for thirty years I have dreamed of being the first to see something so beautiful. Now I need to dream no more."

ALBERT FALCO,
pilot of the mini-sub *Soucoupe*,
upon seeing the figurehead of *Hamilton*
in 1980.

THE CAPSIZING OF *HAMILTON* AND *SCOURGE* CAUSED THE largest single loss of life on the lakes during the War of 1812. Accounts of the tragedy were widely published in newspapers of the day. The *Buffalo Gazette* of August 17 reported:

> It is with deep regret that we record the following facts: about 2 o'clock on Sunday morning last, a most dreadful accident happened in Commodore Chauncey's squadron off Forty Mile Creek on Lake Ontario; the schooners *General* [sic] *Hamilton*, Lieut. Winter, and *Scourge*, Sailing Master Osgood, were upset and lost . . .
>
> The gale lasted but a few minutes and did not affect the ships but injured some of the schooners' sails. Boats were put out from two of the schooners, which succeeded in rescuing about a dozen of the crews. The *Hamilton* having nine guns, the *Scourge*, ten. In a moment 100 [sic] of our brave fellows were plunged into the wave, and two of our best schooners lost to the service.

Another account stated that: "The squall was accompanied with heavy hail and rain and the most vivid flashes of lightning ever witnessed in this latitude."

Nor did interest wane. On October 24, 1815, William and James Crooks, "formerly of Niagara, Merchants," claimed for loss sustained by the enemy: "For a new Schooner, Burthen about fifty tons, call'd the *Lord Nelson* captured by the Brig *Oneida*, Lieut. Woolsey on the 5th June 1812, whilst on her passage from Prescott, to Niagara, £1,000 . . . Halifax Currency."

The United States brought the libel to trial on July 11, 1817: a decree was then made by the Court of the Northern District of New York that pronounced the seizure illegal, and directed that the proceeds of the sale be paid to the Crooks brothers.

However, bizarre though it may seem, Theron Rudd, clerk of that court, had in the meantime absconded with all the funds of the court, so the owners did not get paid.

The circumstance triggered nearly constant legal and political pressure by James and William Crooks and their heirs. James Crooks was in a good position to exert political pressure: a pioneer industrialist and miller, he was twice elected to the Upper Canadian House of Assembly, and, in 1831, appointed Member of the Legislative Council of Upper Canada. He was reappointed to the Legislative Council of the United Parliaments in 1841, an appointment he held until his death in 1860. William, a respected merchant, also participated in the pursuit of repayment which was frustrating even though they found no lack of sympathy in high places. In fact, the Crooks presented their claim to the United States government and Congress, and at different times this received the approval of the Executive, the Senate, the House of Representatives, and numerous House

James Crooks, part-owner of *Lord Nelson* (later *Scourge*) when she was captured thirteen days before war was declared, was a pioneer industrialist and, after the War of 1812 he was twice elected to the Upper Canadian House of Assembly, and, in 1831, appointed Member of the Legislative Council of Upper Canada. He was reappointed to the Legislative Council of the United Parliaments in 1841, an appointment he held until his death in 1860. The Crooks family claim for reparation was finally settled in 1930.

James Fenimore Cooper was at the peak of his popularity when he published (in 1843) Ned Myers's account of his service in *Scourge*. New editions were published in 1852, 1857, 1860, and 1899; the work was also translated into French and German.

committees. It was twice recommended to the favourable consideration of Congress in messages from the president, first by President Monroe in 1819, and again by President Cleveland (the cause having been taken over by the Crooks descendants) in April 1886.

Finally, in 1927, the United States government paid to the Canadian government $23,644.38; after deduction of arbitration and legal expenses, payment of $15,546.63 was made in 1930 to twenty-five beneficiaries, selected from more than one hundred claimants and, with newspaper fanfare, the case was closed.

In the meantime, James Fenimore Cooper's *Ned Myers; or a Life Before the Mast* was published in 1843 when Cooper was at the full flood of his popularity; new editions were published in rapid succession; also, the work was translated into French and German. Furthermore, the capture of *Lord Nelson* was the

The capture of *Lord Nelson* was the subject of a popular painting by C.H.J. Snider, celebrated newspaperman and author of a swashbuckling account of naval warfare on the lakes in which the schooner's capture and capsizing was featured. Published in England, Canada and the United States (1913, revised edition, 1926), the account provided thrilling reading for two generations of boys.

subject of a popular painting by C.H.J. Snider, whose swashbuckling book about naval warfare on the lakes entitled *In the Wake of the Eighteen-Twelvers* was first published in 1913; a revised edition was published in 1926. Snider, a celebrated newspaperman, artist, and author specializing in maritime life on the lakes, concocted a ghostly vision of *Scourge*: "The shadow ship seemed a small two-masted schooner.... She throbbed with a dull blue glare." He follows with an account of her capture as *Lord Nelson* and the trunks found on board. There is also a thrilling graphic description of the capsizing of both *Hamilton* and *Scourge*. This exciting volume of popular history was favourite reading for a couple of generations of North American boys, and can still be read with pleasure today.

The existence of *Hamilton* and *Scourge* was therefore known, as was their approximate location, but because of the depth of the water, search or exploration was for years merely a dream.

This was perhaps just as well, because the discipline of underwater archaeology developed only after the invention of the aqualung by Jacques Cousteau and Emile Gagnan in the 1940s; this enabled the systematic exploration of nautical sites. The formal techniques of nautical archaeology were pioneered in the 1950s, particularly by the American George Bass and his colleagues.

The Swedish Museum of Maritime History was the first in

His Majesty's Schooner *Sauk*, originally an American merchant schooner, was built at the Niagara River above the falls in 1809. She served in the United States Navy on the upper lakes until captured by a British boarding party in August, 1814. Until the discovery of *Hamilton* and *Scourge*, this painting was a unique portrait record of a lakes schooner constructed in pioneering days, a time crucial to the development of two great nations and peoples.

the world to list the new marine archaeology as one of its regular activities; in connection with this, Anders Franzén, chief engineering secretary for the Swedish Admiralty and a marine archaeologist by avocation, set out to find the famous and partly salvaged royal warship *Wasa* at the bottom of Stockholm Harbour. In August, 1956, her location and identity were confirmed; raising her was a five-year cooperative effort on the part of many sectors of the Swedish government and private industry. She has since become the most popular tourist attraction in the Scandinavian countries.

The preservation technology pioneered by *Wasa*'s conservators was developed further by the Danish National Museum which, in 1947, had initiated a search in Roskilde Fjord for the legendary medieval "Queen Margrethe's ship." The unsuccessful search led two young sports divers, Aage Skjelborg and Hartvig Conradsen, to search further. Their Viking finds persuaded the National Museum to continue, and in July, 1957, that institution commenced one of the world's major maritime archaeology projects, the excavation and reclamation (by an army of students), and subsequent preservation and spectacular display of five Viking ships that had been scuttled to block the harbour entrance. Waterlogged-wood conservation techniques pioneered and developed on this project by Børge Brorson Christensen set a world standard for the field, extended by continuing work in Stockholm and by those working on the meticulous repair and conservation of the medieval cog at Bremerhaven in Germany.

In 1967, the *Mary Rose* Committee was formed to "find, excavate, raise and preserve for all time such remains of the ship *Mary Rose* as may be of historical and archaeological interest." This action was an outgrowth of journalist and amateur diver Alexander McKee's search for wrecks of interest in the Solent on the south coast of England. Archaeologist Margaret Rule was one of the charter members of that committee: since 1971, when the find of Henry VIII's flagship was confirmed, she has been a guiding force in the eleven-year excavation, and the raising of the remaining portion of the hull; this has transformed our understanding of maritime life in sixteenth-century England. The undertaking has also involved vast numbers of volunteers, extensive support by private industry and co-operation from many government agencies.

In 1971, through the office of Dr. A. Douglas Tushingham at the Royal Ontario Museum in Toronto, the *Hamilton-Scourge* Project was initiated. The driving force behind the search for and subsequent investigation of the two schooners was Dr. Daniel A. Nelson, a dentist from St. Catharines, Ontario, a diver and a keen amateur archaeologist. Using the primary records of Myers's account and the *Wolfe* log, he delineated a search area. As interest in the schooners grew, a group of scientists and technologists became involved, particularly Dr. Peter Sly and others from the Canada Centre for Inland Waters in Burlington, Ontario.

Preliminary search-trials were conducted in 1972 in the "most likely" area near the south shore of Lake Ontario to the west of the Niagara River. In the fall of 1973, magnetometer and side-scan sonar-grid surveys were carried out by several cooperating agencies. At this time, a likely "target" was indicated on the lake floor.

A few days later, Captain Archie Hodge, who had captained the search vessel during previous investigations, was travelling home in his ship. It was a calm November evening, and he decided to put down the sonar to search for *Hamilton* and *Scourge*. He picked up a target, and accomplished a pre-arranged cross-referencing pattern, which picked up a second target; this gave later researchers more precise investigatory documentation.

In 1975, during deep-tow side-scan trials of new equipment, researchers first saw images of the two vessels, upright on the lake floor, with hulls intact, masts, topmasts, and bowsprits in place, and strong reflectors on the deck in locations where one could expect guns had been situated, thus enabling nearly certain identification of the ships.

Later that year, in November, earlier interpretations of side-scan records were verified during field trials of a remote-control vehicle that carried a television camera. Viewed at this time were *Hamilton's* ship's boat, a platter, spars, some bones, and cannon-balls (which conclusively dated the vessel, and thus confirmed its identity). Because of the apparently near-perfect condition of the schooner, the video record caused international excitement. It was evident that at least one schooner was an archaeological discovery of great importance, evidently perfectly preserved with all artifacts in fresh water, utter darkness, and near-freezing temperatures.

Advanced acoustic survey methods were developed using *Hamilton* and *Scourge* as subjects. The extensive study resulted in sophisticated sonar images of both ships, which enabled researchers to hypothesize deck plans and dimensions; considerable data was gathered concerning the environment in which the schooners lie.

During the early period of exploration, title to the ships rested with the United States Navy. In 1978, however, the navy received the acquiescence of the United States Congress to transfer title. It was at that time that, due to the enthusiasm of Mayor John A. MacDonald and Alderman William M. McCulloch, both Royal Canadian Navy veterans (and the latter a keen amateur historian), the City of Hamilton, Ontario stepped forward and offered to take title to the ships and to coordinate the international-level archaeological project.

Accordingly, as a first step, in April 1979, title to the ships was transferred by the Department of the Navy to the Royal

Ontario Museum. In June of the same year, the city moved to execute the agreement with the Royal Ontario Museum (and with the United States government, represented by the navy), "respecting two ships," which would transfer title to the city.

Comprehensive private legislation of the provincial legislature (The City of Hamilton Act, 1979) enabled the city to pass by-laws relating to all aspects of the study, raising, display, and restoration of *Hamilton* and *Scourge* and their artifacts. After Ontario Municipal Board approval was received, the city was finally free on May 1, 1980 to take title.

In the summer of 1980, Jacques Cousteau arranged for the photography of *Hamilton*; at the time Albert Falco, seasoned pilot of the mini-sub *Soucoupe*, exclaimed after seeing *Diana*'s figurehead that in thirty years of diving he had often dreamed of being the first to see something so beautiful. "Now I need dream no more."

In 1981, the City of Hamilton created The *Hamilton* and *Scourge*, Foundation, Inc., a non-profit corporation for the purpose of project fund-raising and disbursement. In the same year, a supporting volunteer organization, the *Hamilton-Scourge* Society, was formed; this group now runs — among a host of other volunteer projects relating to the schooners — a speakers' bureau whose members travel far and wide to satisfy intense public interest.

In May, 1982, the foundation co-operated with the National Geographic Society in an extensive survey of both vessels, which resulted in nineteen hundred still pictures and twenty-six hours of videotape. *Scourge* was seen for the first time, and researchers could appreciate the unique qualities of each schooner. The photographs of *Hamilton* and *Scourge* in this book are all Emory Kristof's photographs, taken at that time; the remote-controlled underwater vehicle used to hold the cameras was the invention of a young American engineer, Chris Nicholson.

In March, 1983, Hamilton City Council created a Special Committee of Council for operational administrative purposes of an extensive task-force and staff structure. Future research plans include the completion of a feasibility study, which will include referenced, detailed, visual recording of all aspects of the ships' materials plus conservation and geotechnical studies. Results will determine the methods by which the schooners will be raised and exhibited. A factor very much in the project's favour is the small size of the schooners. *Hamilton's* length, upon the range of the deck, is approximately seventy-three feet; that of *Scourge* is thought to be fifty-seven feet. Both ships are approximately twenty feet wide amidships. Other positive factors are the schooners' undamaged condition, and their excellent state of preservation: we can infer, from the position of the ordnance, that *Scourge* and *Hamilton*, when they capsized, turned on their port beam-ends, and, once below the surface of the water, ballasted by their armament, righted and drifted by means of their sails to the bottom of the lake, approximately three hundred feet below. They came to rest fifteen hundred feet apart on the soft clay silt of the lake floor. The lake bed is flat and featureless near the ships. No destructive light penetrates so deep into the lake; the fresh, preserving water is at a constant, near-freezing temperature; currents are gentle.

Also greatly in the project's favour is the site chosen for their display. The Regional Municipality of Hamilton-Wentworth, through the Hamilton Region Conservation Authority, has set aside a magnificent five-acre site in the heart of a five-hundred-acre park on the shore of Lake Ontario close by Canada's most-travelled highway system, the Queen Elizabeth Way, which joins the northern belt of states with the Province of Ontario.

Hamilton and *Scourge* are archaeological and historical treasures of international importance, yet they are appropriate symbols of their time and place and, today, have wonderful appeal because of their sturdy ordinariness. These are not large and specialized vessels such as *Wasa* and *Mary Rose*. Rather, they are "people's ships," essential to the development of the western world in the long, early days of the industrial revolution, when production volume of many small factories and raw materials sources was small, and distances between these and their widely spaced small markets were great.

Schooners like *Hamilton* and *Scourge* once plied the North and Irish Seas; they sailed along the coasts of England, Scotland, Wales, Denmark, Australia, and New Zealand. They were particularly useful along the east coast of North America and in the Caribbean. They were produced in great numbers for export from Canada's maritimes. Because of their ability to move easily in and out of narrow, shallow harbours and river-mouths, and to head-up off a lee shore, they were much used for merchant traffic on the Great Lakes and particularly on Lake Ontario.

Although — or perhaps because — they were so ordinary, very little documentation remains of these early small schooners. To find two, perfectly preserved, one Canadian, one American, dating from pioneering days, a time crucial to the development of our two nations — is an extraordinary gift. They are an invaluable legacy for two great nations and peoples.

NOTES

PART ONE

PAGE LINE

19　13　"A Canadian Boat Song" in *The Poetical Works of Thomas Moore* (Paris, 1829), pp. 116-17.

19　25　George Heriot, *Travels Through the Canadas*. 2 vols. (London: Richard Phillips, 1807), 1: 173.

20　13　Joseph Bouchette, *The British Dominions in North America*. 2 vols. (London: Longman, 1832), 1: 89n.

20　25　*Mrs. Simcoe's Diary*, ed. Mary Quayle Innis (Toronto: Macmillan, 1965). Entry for Friday, June 10, 1796.

21　11　Lieutenant F. Elmer, from Anthony M. Slosek, *Oswego: Hamlet Days 1796–1828* (Oswego, 1980), p. 8.

22　19　*Mrs. Simcoe's Diary*, Friday, July 13, 1792.

22　24　Heriot, 1: 156.

23　21　Hannah Peters Jarvis to Samuel Peters, August 15, 1810. MG 23 H I 3 vol. 2, no. 196, Public Archives of Canada.

24　8　Isaac Weld, *Travels Through the States of North America and the Provinces of Upper and Lower Canada During the Years 1795, 1796, and 1797*. 2 vols. Fourth edition. (London: 1807), 2, p. 68.

24　10　Ibid, 73.

24　25　Slosek, 38.

24　28　Deputy Surveyor-General Collins in his report to Lord Dorchester, 1788, in volume 2, John Ross Robertson, *Landmarks of Toronto*. 6 vols. (Toronto: J. Ross Robertson, 1896), p. 821.

24　38　Ibid.

24　46　Ibid.

26　7　Ibid.

26　18　Weld, 2: 72.

26　20　*Mrs. Simcoe's Diary*, Monday, July 23, 1792.

26　27　*Mrs. Simcoe's Diary*, Friday, April 29, 1796.

26　32　The "Devil's Nose" was thirty-five miles due west of the Genesee River.

27	9	Heriot, 1: 132.
28	35	Joseph Willcocks to Sir Richard Willcocks. From W.R. Riddell, *Life of John Graves Simcoe* (Toronto: McClelland and Stewart, 1926), p. 292.
29	2	Heriot, 1: 130-31.
29	8	Weld, 2: 66.
29	17	Heriot, 1: 131.
30	6	Statistical data concerning Provincial Marine and Royal Navy vessels on Lake Ontario from C.P. Stacey, "The Ships of the British Squadron on Lake Ontario, 1812–14," in *The Canadian Historical Review*, 34 (1953), 311-23.
30	13	Heriot, 1: 131.
31	21	Ibid, 117-18.
32	10	Ibid, 154.
32	25	Mary Agnes FitzGibbon, "The Jarvis Letters." In *Family History* (Niagara-on-the-Lake: Niagara Historical Society, 1901, 1982), Publication no. 8, p. 29.
32	43	Ibid, 35.
33	32	Heriot, 1: 149-57.
34	17	H.A. Innis, "From Outpost to Empire: An Introduction to the Economic History of Ontario." *Ontario Historical Society Papers and Records*, 30 (1934), 119.
34	27	Ernest Green, "The Niagara Portage Road." *Ontario Historical Society Papers and Records*, 23 (1926), 278.
35	1	*Mrs. Simcoe's Diary*, Monday, July 30, 1792.
35	9	Heriot, 1: 159-61.
35	18	*Mrs. Simcoe's Diary*, Monday, July 30, 1792.
36	3	Bruce Wilson, "A Study of the Enterprises of Robert Hamilton." Ph.D. diss., University of Toronto, 1978, p. 185.
36	5	In 1803, Ramsay Crooks, a sixteen-year-old younger brother, followed his older siblings to North America. He travelled to the west coast as part of John Jacob Astor's Pacific Fur Company expedition, which established, in 1811, the post of Astoria on the Columbia River. Ramsay later became president of Astor's American Fur Company in New York upon Astor's retirement in 1834.

37	11	James Fenimore Cooper, *Lives of Distinguished American Naval Officers* (Auburn, N.Y.: Derby, 1846), p. 126.
37	31	Excerpt from "The Foresters: A Poem description of a Pedestrian Journey to the Falls of Niagara in the Autumn of 1804" by Alexander Wilson, author of *American Ornithology*, ll. 1869–86. From *The Poems and Literary Prose of Alexander Wilson* ed. Rev. Alexander B. Grosart (Paisley: 1876), pp. 163-64.
38	14	F. Hosmer Culkin, "Alvin Bronson, A First Citizen of Oswego." *Oswego County Historical Society Publication*, 14 (1951), 69.
38	39	Cooper, *Lives*, 126.
38	40	W.A.B. Douglas, "The Anatomy of Naval Incompetence: The Provincial Marine in Defence of Upper Canada Before 1813." *Ontario History*, 71 (1979), 24, 35 n.
39	5	Cooper, *Lives*, 128.
39	5	For a picture of *Oneida* see page 91. Interestingly, when *Oneida* was built, the spaces between her frames were filled with salt, as a perservative measure. The British ship, *Earl of Moira*, built at Kingston in 1805, was treated the same way. In relation to salt, in the late 18th century on Lake Ontario there was a prejudice against "Oswego" salt because it was thought to turn the pork blue; British army regulars objected to this.
39	20	Franklin B. Hough, *A History of Jefferson County in the State of New York* (Albany: Munsell, 1854), p. 459. The Oswegatchie is at Ogdensburg on the St. Lawrence; Sandy Creek lies approximately halfway between Sackets Harbor and Oswego on the east coast of Lake Ontario.
39	43	Susan Fenimore Cooper, *The Cooper Gallery or Pages and Pictures* (New York: Miller, 1865), p. 309.
40	6	*Oswego Daily Times*, Wednesday, January 27, 1858, and *Oswego Palladium*, Wednesday, January 27, 1858: obituaries of Henry Eagle.
52	3	Dana Story, *Hail Columbia!* (Barre, Mass.: Barre Publishers, 1970), pp. 64-82. This excerpt has been edited to delete inconsequential material and, like other excerpts in the book, some modification has been made for the modern reader. Note: "Hackmatack" is an Indian word for American larch; a "knee" is a naturally-carved timber used for a brace in ship construction.
53	26	Woolsey to Hamilton, July 23, 1811. Records of the Office of Naval Records and Library (RG-45), *Officers' Letters*, 1811. National Archives.
53	41	Woolsey to Hamilton, September 14, 1811.
54	2	Woolsey to Hamilton, November 29, 1811.

54	19	Woolsey to Hamilton, May 4, 1812.
55	4	Woolsey to Hamilton, June 9, 1812. Also on board the *Lord Nelson* was Robert Emery, a thirteen-year-old "apprenticed to the owner . . . to learn the art of navigation." After the capture, Woolsey sent him to school at Sacket's Harbor. From *In the Court of Claims*, p. 44.
55	19	James Crooks, "Recollections of the War of 1812." In *Family History and Reminiscences of Early Settlers*, Niagara Historical Society Publication, no. 28, p. 30.
56	9	Records of the Office of Naval Records and Library (RG-45), *Commanders' Letters*, 1813. Deposition by Alexander Darragh, given to William Baker, Esq., Justice of the Peace, Jefferson County, May 17, 1813.

The general instructions under which Woolsey made seizure of *Lord Nelson* were to "advise and co-operate with the collector of the Customs. The proper objects of seizure, are all vessels acting or found under such circumstances as may satisfy a strong suspicion of their intention to act in violation of this law [the new Embargo Act, passed April 4, 1812]. In enforcing this law, we are not to violate the territorial jurisdiction of a foreign state. All vessels seized under this law are to be sent into port for adjudication; the papers found on board of them are to be placed in the hands of the district attorney, who will thereupon proceed according to law."

Secretary of the Navy Paul Hamilton to Woolsey, April 8, 1812. ("Statement of the Seizure of the British Schooner *Lord Nelson*, by an American Vessel of War on the 5th June, 1812." Hamilton: Journal and Express Office, 1841. Pamphlet, page 12.)

Governor General of the Canadas and Commander in Chief of His Majesty's Forces, Sir George Prevost, commented in a letter dated June 14, 1812: "a most extraordinary circumstance . . . occurred on Lake Ontario in the 5th inst. . . . A British vessel, the *Lord Nelson*, loaded in part with merchandise for Queenston and Niagara and about fifty miles below that port . . . was brought to by firing of three guns at her. . . . The reason given for taking this vessel are that she was found without either register or Custom House clearance on board. The Laws of Upper Canada do not require (this)."

(Extract, no correspondent given: MG 11, CO 42, vol. 146, pp. 249-50, Public Archives of Canada.)

There are discrepancies in the inventories of *Lord Nelson*'s cargo at the time of her capture. Perhaps the more reliable can be derived from James Crooks's record of invoices and evaluations. *In the Court of Claims*, 25.
16 bars iron
68 bars flat iron
15 bars axe iron
4 bundles scythes
2 barrels and one trunk containing dry goods

　　　　　　3 iron-bound barrels of Jamaica spirits
　　　　　　1 iron-bound barrel of Teneriffe wine
　　　　　　3 boxes glass (50 feet each)
　　　　　　1 keg powder (50 pounds)
　　　　　　1 keg linseed oil (6 gallons)
　　　　　　two or three crates of crockery
　　　　　　seven trunks containing bedding and the apparel of a lady
　　　　　　1 bedstead

　　　　　　Total estimated value in 1812:
　　　　　　£759　34　9½

56　　18　Gilkison Papers, MS 497, Ontario Archives.

57　　 6　Woolsey to Jones, May 12, 1813.

PART TWO

58　　14　A.T. Mahan, *Seapower in its Relation to the War of 1812*. 2 vols. (London: Sampson, Low, 1905), 1, p. 298. Mahan gives no reference for this quotation.

60　　23　Miss Butler, "Historical Facts Regarding Sackets Harbor and Madison Barracks with Side Lights on the War of 1812." Pamphlet, undated, unpaged, ca. 1900.

60　　31　Woolsey to Hamilton, July 21, 1812.

60　　39　Abstract from Chauncey's journal sent to Secretary of the Navy Paul Hamilton, September 26, 1812.

60　　45　Woolsey to Hamilton, September 7, 1812.

61　　 3　Chauncey to Hamilton, September 26, 1812.

62　　10　James Fenimore Cooper, *Ned Myers: or A Life Before The Mast* (New York: Stringer and Townshend, 1852), pp. 46-48.

62　　15　Chauncey to Hamilton, October 8, 1812.

63　　23　Woolsey to Hamilton, October 6, 1812.

63　　33　Darragh deposition. See notes from Part One, page 56, line 9.

63　　34　Woolsey to Hamilton, October 6, 1812.

63　　37　Chauncey to Hamilton, October 8, 1812.

63　　44　Ibid.

64　　22　Cooper, *Myers*, 48-49.

64	38	Prevost to Brock, September 25, 1812. In E.A. Cruikshank, *The Documentary History of the Campaign upon the Niagara Frontier*. 9 vols. (Welland: Tribune Office, 1902–1908), 3, p. 295.
64	49	Chauncey to Hamilton, October 21, 1812.
65	5	Chauncey to Hamilton, November 4, 1812.
65	10	Records of the Office of Naval Records and Library (RG-45), Roster of Vessels and Yards, 1811–1827. National Archives.
65	13	Chauncey to Hamilton, November 5, 1812.
66	2	Chauncey to Hamilton, November 6, 1812.
67	11	Cooper, *Myers*, 49.
68	4	Chauncey to Hamilton, November 13, 1812.
68	12	Ibid. The attack was actually made on November 10, 1812. In relation to American losses during the attack on Kingston, Chauncey stated: "We lost in this affair [in the *Oneida*] 1 man killed and 3 slightly wounded, with a few shot through our sails. The other vessels lost no men and received but little injury to their hull and sails with the exception of the *Pert*, whose gun bursted in the early part of the action and wounded her Commander (Sailing Master Arundel) badly, and a midshipman and 3 men slightly. Mr. Arundel who refused to quit the Deck although wounded, was knocked overboard in beating up to our anchorage and I am sorry to say was drowned." For a full description of the attack on Kingston see, C.P. Stacey, "Commodore Chauncey's Attack on Kingston Harbour, November 10, 1812." In *The Canadian Historical Review*, 32 (1951), 126-38.
68	21	Cooper, *Myers*, 49-50.
68	25	Chauncey to Hamilton, November 17, 1812.
70	6	*Kingston Gazette*, November 17, 1812. In J. Douglas Stewart and Ian F. Wilson, *Heritage Kingston* (Exhibition catalogue, Agnes Etherington Arts Centre, Queen's University at Kingston, Ontario, 1973), p. 57.
70	16	Chauncey to Hamilton, November 13, 1812.
71	5	Chauncey to Hamilton, November 17, 1812.
71	18	Chauncey to Hamilton, November 22, 1812.
71	23	Chauncey to Hamilton, December 12, 1812.
71	30	Cooper, *Myers*, 50.

72	9	Chauncey to Jones, February 21, 1813.
72	23	David Wingfield, "Four Years on the Lakes of Canada." Ms., p. 6. Manuscript group 24, F18, Public Archives of Canada.
72	31	Cooper, *Myers*, 50-51.
72	35	Wingfield, 6.
72	41	Chauncey to Hamilton, December 8, 1812.
72	43	Cooper, *Myers*, 46.
73	14	Woolsey to Hamilton, March 15, 1812. These were the ingredients of the naval rations.
73	31	Records of the Office of Naval Records and Library (RG-45) SNL, vol. 10, 58. National Archives. From the proofs of volume 1 (of three) of the forthcoming publication *The Naval War of 1812: A Documentary History* (Washington: Naval Historical Center).
73	35	Cooper, *Myers*, 50.
76	35	Captain Andrew Gray to Governor-General Prevost, January 19, 1813. In Cruikshank, 5: 43-44.
77	42	Jones to Chauncey, January 27, 1813.
78	11	For a concise description of the American ship-building programme on Lake Erie, see Max Rosenberg, *The Building of Perry's Fleet on Lake Erie, 1812–1813* (Harrisburg: Pennsylvania Historical and Museum Commission, 1974). This pamphlet has a bibliography for further reading. The Canadian ship-building programme at Amherstburg is described in a corresponding pamphlet, *Ship-building at Fort Amherstburg 1796–1813* (Ottawa, Parks Canada, 1978). Ref. QS-C041-000-BB-A1.
79	6	Lieutenant Angus to Chauncey, December 25, 1812, as enclosed in Chauncey to Jones, April 2, 1813.
		Lieutenant Angus was about to punish a man in what Chauncey "deemed an improper manner," i.e. severely, and in a fit of temper. Chauncey remonstrated with him. Lieutenant Angus then "refused to do any more duty on this station"; evidently he felt undermined in his command. In the case of Captain Leonard, he and Chauncey had fallen out previous to the War of 1812, over a matter of prestige, and an ugly conflict ensued on the lakes.
79	32	Woolsey to Jones, February 20, 1813.
81	13	Bathurst to Prevost, March 12, 1813. In Cruikshank, 5: 105-07.

84	6	Cooper, *Myers*, 51.
84	49	Ibid, 51-53.
85	15	Ibid, 55-56.
88	4	Chauncey to Jones, May 7, 1813.
88	9	Cooper, *Myers*, 56.
88	17	Chauncey to Jones, May 11, 1813.
88	20	Cooper, *Myers*, 56.
88	27	Woolsey to Jones, May 12, 1813.
89	2	Woolsey to Thomas McCormick, September 22, 1815. *In the Court of Claims*, p. 30.
89	11	Chauncey to Jones, May 15, 1813.
89	30	Yeo to the Honourable John Wilson Croker, May 26, 1813. In Cruikshank, 5: 244.
90	13	Chauncey to Jones, May 28, 1813.
90	37	Quoted in Alex. Slidell Mackenzie, *The Life of Commodore Oliver Hazard Perry*. 2 vols. (New York: Harpers, 1840) 1, 141-44.
91	3	Cooper, *Myers*, 56.
91	13	Chauncey to Jones, May 28, 1813.
91	27	Cooper, *Myers*, 56-57.
92	5	Chauncey to Jones, May 28, 1813.
92	10	Captain Fowler, D.A.Q.M.G., to Colonel Baynes, May 29, 1813. In Cruikshank, 5: 258.
92	19	Chauncey to Jones, May 28, 1813.
94	8	Wingfield, 6-10.
95	2	Ibid.
95	5	Chauncey to Jones, June 2, 1813.
96	12	Yeo to Croker, June 29, 1813. In Cruikshank, 6: 160.
96	23	Woolsey to Chauncey, June 19, 1813.
96	37	Yeo to Hon. John Wilson Croker, July 16, 1813. In Cruikshank, 6: 245.

97   17   Roster: see notes for page 65, line 10 above.

An approximate idea of the weight of the guns on the decks of *Hamilton* and *Scourge* can be derived from Louis de Tousard's *American Artillerist's Companion* (2 vols., Philadelphia, 1809). Two alternate weights are given for 18-pounder "English Carronades": 1,008 and 949 pounds (vol. 2, p. 386). The weight given for a 12-pounder long gun is 2,995 pounds, and for a 6-pounder long gun, 1,733 pounds (vol. 1, p. 140). The latter table lacks a weight for 4-pounder long guns.

97   23   Records of the Office of Naval Records and Library (RG-45). Muster rolls of *Hamilton* and *Scourge*, National Archives.

PART THREE

98   18   Chauncey to Jones, August 13, 1813.

99   13   Yeo to Prevost, August 9, 1813. In Cruikshank, 6: 327.

99   23   Chauncey to Jones, August 13, 1813.

100   13   Cooper, *Myers*, 63.

100   22   Chauncey to Jones, August 13, 1813.

110   49   Records of the Office of Naval Records and Library (RG-45): *Wolfe* log, Sunday, August 8, 1813. National Archives.

111   4   Yeo to Prevost, August 9, 1813. In Cruikshank, 6: 327.

112   10   Chauncey to Jones, August 13, 1813.

116   50   Yeo to Prevost, August 11, 1813. In Cruikshank, 7: 7-8.

117   11   Chauncey to Jones, August 13, 1813.

117   25   Yeo to Prevost, August 9, 1813. In Cruikshank, 6: 327-28.

PART FOUR

124   8   Tape recording of dive on *Hamilton* by *Soucoupe*, 1980; quoted from Eric McGuinness, "Voyage Through a Time Tunnel." *Dofasco Illustrated News*, vol. 45, no. 5 (1981), 2.

125   15   *Buffalo Gazette*, August 17, 1813. In Cruikshank 34: 26.

125   18   *United States Gazette*, August 27, 1813. In Cruikshank 7: 26.

125   25   R 619 E5 (a) vol. 3740, Public Archives of Canada.

125   32   Theron Rudd absconded with $123, 884.44. Suspicion was also cast upon his assistant. *In the Court of Claims*, p. 15.

125	38	The Legislative Council was established as the provincial equivalent to the House of Lords, and had the functions of an Upper House.
126	7	Memorial of His Britanic Majesty's Government, Pecuniary Claims Commission, The "*Lord Nelson*", prepared for debate on March 26, 1914. Payment of $5,000 was allowed, with simple interest at 4%, calculated from February 3, 1819 to April 26, 1912.
126	15	Ned Myers was published simultaneously in England and the United States in 1843. An English-language edition and a French-language edition were published in Paris followed in 1844. Four American editions followed, in 1849, 1850, 1851 and 1852. In 1853 the book was republished in London; 1857 and 1860 saw new American editions. In 1862 the book was published in Germany in German, and a final American edition was published *circa* 1899. (*The National Union Catalogue Pre-1956 Imprints*, vol. 121, p. 632.)
127	7	C.H.J. Snider, *In the Wake of the Eighteen-Twelvers, Fights and Flights of Frigates and Fore-'n-afters in the War of 1812-1815 on the Great Lakes*. (London: John Lane, The Bodley Head; New York: John Lane Company; Toronto: Bell & Cockburn, 1913). Revised and reprinted in 1926 as: *The Story of the "Nancy" and other Eighteen-Twelvers*, (Toronto: McClelland & Stewart, 1926).
130	23	Margaret Rule, *The Mary Rose: The Excavation and Raising of Henry VIII's Flagship* (London: Conway, 1983), p. 54.
132	16	See page 124, line 8, above.
132	45	These preliminary estimates of length and width are derived from: Kenneth A. Cassavoy "*Hamilton/Scourge* May 1982 Survey, Preliminary Archaeological Report, October, 1982." Mimeographed. (Hamilton, Ontario: The *Hamilton-Scourge* Foundation, Inc., 1982.)

LIST OF ILLUSTRATIONS

Maps   Page

Districts in the Province of Upper Canada, by William Chewitt. Published by William Faden, London, 1813. / Archives of Ontario, Toronto, Canada — 14–15

The Provinces of Upper and Lower Canada, by Joseph Bouchette. Published by William Faden, London, 1815. / National Map Collection, Public Archives of Canada, Ottawa [0018392 (2 sect.)] — 23

Fortifications at Sackets Harbor, 1814, by F.P. Robinson, A.D.C. / National Map Collection, Public Archives of Canada, Ottawa (H12/1240) — 94

Plates

Betsey: American schooner built 1799. / Peabody Museum of Salem. Photo by Mark Sexton. — 16

View of St. Augustin, by George Heriot. / Picture Division, Public Archives of Canada, Ottawa (C-12769) — 18

King's Head Inn, Burlington Bay, Ontario, June 11, 1796, by Elizabeth Simcoe. / Picture Division, Public Archives of Canada, Ottawa (C-13914) — 20

View of Fort Niagara, ca. 1783, by James Peachy. / Picture Division, Public Archives of Canada, Ottawa (C-2035) — 21

Encampment of the Loyalists, 1784, by James Peachy. / Picture Division, Public Archives of Canada, Ottawa (C-2001) — 22

Ship's compass. From: David Steel, *The Elements and Practice of Rigging and Seamanship*. 2 vols. (London: David Steel, 1794). / Courtesy Essex Institute, Salem, Mass. — 25

Fort Cataraqui (Kingston), 1783, by James Peachy. / Picture Division, Public Archives of Canada, Ottawa (C-2301 detail) — 26

View of York, 1804, by Elizabeth F. Hale. / Picture Division, Public Archives of Canada, Ottawa (C-34334) — 27, top

York Barracks, by Lt. Sempronius Stretton. / Picture Division, Public Archives of Canada, Ottawa (C-14905) — 27, bottom

View of Cataraqui (Kingston), 1784, by James Peachy. / Picture Division, Public Archives of Canada, Ottawa (C-1512) — 29

Mr. Secretary Wm. Jarvis and son Samuel Peters Jarvis, 1792. / Courtesy of the Royal Ontario Museum, Toronto, Ontario — 30

Hannah Peters Jarvis, with eldest daughters Maria Lavinia and Augusta Honoria. / Courtesy of the Royal Ontario Museum, Toronto, Canada — 31

Queenston, 1805, by George Heriot. / Picture Division, Public Archives of Canada, Ottawa (C-12772) — 33

The Falls of Niagara, by George Heriot. / Picture Division, Public Archives of Canada, Ottawa (C-12797) — 34

View of Fort Erie, by E. Walsh. / Courtesy of the Royal Ontario Museum, Toronto, Canada — 35

View of Fort Oswego. / Courtesy Anthony M. Slosek	32
Melancthon Taylor Woolsey, by Abraham G.D. Tuthill, ca. 1820. / Courtesy of the New-York Historical Society, New York City	38
Federal George, American schooner built 1794. / Peabody Museum of Salem, Mass. Photo by Mark Sexton	43, top
Petrel, American schooner built 1815. / Peabody Museum of Salem, Mass. Photo by Mark Sexton	43, bottom
H.H. Cole, American schooner built 1843, by Clement Drew. / Peabody Museum of Salem, Mass. Photo by Mark Sexton	44–45
President James Madison, by Gilbert Stuart. / Bowdoin College Museum of Art, Brunswick, Maine	59
Major-General Sir Isaac Brock, by George Theodore Berthon. / Government of Ontario Art Collection, Queen's Park, Toronto, Canada	62
Commodore Isaac Chauncey, by Gilbert Stuart, ca. 1818. / U.S. Naval Academy collection	63
Henry Eckford, from a painting in the possession of the Long Island Historical Society. / Courtesy of Richard Palmer	64
"McDonough Pointing the Gun," by J.R. Chapin and F.F. Walker, published 1859. / Courtesy of the author	69
Sir James Lucas Yeo, by A. Buck, published 1810. / Metropolitan Toronto Library, T15241, Toronto, Canada	78
Navy Yard, Amherstburg, by Margaret Reynolds, 1813. / Fort Malden National Historic Park, Parks Canada	86–87
Death of American General Zebulon Pike on April 27, 1813. / Picture Division, Public Archives of Canada, Ottawa (C-7434)	88
Capture of Fort George, May 27, 1813. / Naval Historical Center, U.S. Navy.	91
Sackets Harbor. Engraving by T. Strickland, published 1815. / Picture Division, Public Archives of Canada, Ottawa (C-8153)	95
Night action, 10th August, 1813, by Master's Mate Peter W. Spicer. / Naval Historical Center, U.S. Navy	114
View of the running fight, 11th September, 1813, by Master's Mate Peter W. Spicer. / Naval Historical Center, U.S. Navy	115
The storming of Fort Oswego, May 6, 1814. / Picture Division, Public Archives of Canada, Ottawa.	118
American privateer schooner *Surprize,* capturing *Star,* January 27, 1815. / Peabody Museum of Salem, Mass. Photo by Mark Sexton	119
Launching of the *St. Lawrence.* / Courtesy of the Royal Ontario Museum, Toronto, Canada	120
Kingston Harbour, July 1815, by Emeric Essex Vidal. / With permission of the Commandant, Royal Military College of Canada, Kingston, Ontario, Canada	120–21
Military post, Sackets Harbor, by J. Milbert. Published, 1826. / Courtesy of the Royal Ontario Museum, Toronto, Canada	122–23

James Fenimore Cooper, published in 1831. / Courtesy of the *Hamilton-Scourge* Foundation, Inc.	126
The capture of the *Lord Nelson* by C.H.J. Snider. / Metropolitan Toronto Library, MTL 1574, Toronto, Canada	127
Sauk, September 15, 1815, by Adam Gordon. / Courtesy of the Royal Ontario Museum, Toronto, Canada	128–29

Photographs

All photographs by Emory Kristof © The *Hamilton* and *Scourge* Foundation, Inc., except where noted.

Figurehead of *Lord Nelson* (*Scourge*).	7
Figurehead of *Diana* (*Hamilton*).	10
Figurehead of *Diana* (*Hamilton*).	40
A schooner model. / By permission of the National Maritime Museum, London, U.K.	41
Beakhead of *Diana* (*Hamilton*).	42, top left
Joining of the bowsprit and jib-boom on *Diana* (*Hamilton*).	42, bottom left
Diana's rudder.	42, top right
Lord Nelson's rudder.	42, bottom right
Story shipyard. / Photo by Dana Story, courtesy Peabody Museum of Salem, Mass.	46, top
Dubbing *Columbia*'s rudder. / Photo by John M. Clayton, courtesy of Peabody Museum of Salem, Mass.	46, bottom left
Dubbing for the garboard strake. / Photo by John M. Clayton, courtesy of Peabody Museum of Salem, Mass.	46, bottom right
Frame-up! / Photo by John M. Clayton, courtesy of Peabody Museum of Salem, Mass.	47, top left
Putting in the deck beams. / Photo by John M. Clayton, courtesy of Peabody Museum of Salem, Mass.	47, top right
Planking *Columbia*. / Photo by John M. Clayton, courtesy of Peabody Museum of Salem, Mass.	47, bottom left
Unfinished deck of *Mayflower*. / Courtesy Peabody Museum of Salem, Mass.	47, bottom right
Cutaway model (two views) of the colonial schooner *Halifax*, by Harold Hahn. / Courtesy of Mr. Hahn	50, 51
Figurehead of *Lord Nelson* (*Scourge*).	55
Shot and axes on board *Scourge*.	65
Long gun, *Scourge*.	66, top
Long gun, *Scourge*.	66, bottom
Carronade, *Hamilton*.	67, top

Carronade, *Hamilton*.	67, bottom
Hamilton's centre pivot-mounted long gun.	68, top left and top right
Hamilton's port cat-head.	74, top
Anchor, *Hamilton*.	74, bottom
Hawse hole and anchor cable, *Scourge*.	75
Pikes lie across *Scourge*'s hatch opening.	82–83
Side-steps on *Scourge*'s starboard side.	85
Grapeshot and objects on *Hamilton*'s port side.	92
Canister: and a dirk which lies on *Hamilton*'s port side.	93
Forward-most port gun, *Scourge*.	99
Pommelion of a portgun on *Scourge*.	100
Rudder post of *Scourge*.	102, top
Hamilton's tiller.	102, bottom
A view of *Scourge*'s deck.	103
Foremast, *Scourge*.	105, top and middle
Sweeps, *Scourge*.	105, bottom
Cabin window, *Scourge*.	106
Views of *Hamilton*'s boat.	107
Fifty-three men died in the sinking of *Hamilton* and *Scourge*.	111
Hon. James Crooks (1778–1860). / Metropolitan Toronto Library, Toronto, Canada	125

Figures

Instructions for cutting ship's timbers. / From Peter Guillet, *The Timber Merchant's Guide*, Baltimore, 1823. Lithograph by Henry Stone. / Courtesy of Peabody Museum of Salem, Mass.	39
An American inventory of Mrs. McCormick's trunks, 1813. / Records of the Office of Naval Records and Library (RG-45), National Archives, Washington, D.C.	56
Broadside published shortly after Brock's triumph at Detroit. / Metropolitan Toronto Library Board, Broadside Collection, Toronto, Canada	61
Undated plan entitled "Iron Guns for the Navy" depicting guns of four- through thirty-six-pounder size. / Naval Historical Center, U.S. Navy	70, 71
Muster rolls of *Hamilton* and *Scourge* from July 1 to August 8, 1813. / Records of the Office of Naval Records and Library (RG-45), National Archives, Washington, D.C.	112 and 113
Entry in *Wolfe*'s log. / Records of the Office of Naval Records and Library (RG-45), National Archives, Washington, D.C.	113, bottom

ACKNOWLEDGEMENTS

The *Hamilton-Scourge* Society, the members of which comprise the volunteer army of the *Hamilton-Scourge* Project, has a tradition of generous co-operation. Of the many members who helped with this particular endeavour, I am especially indebted to Hamilton Alderman William M. McCulloch, for making available to me the results of his research in the National Archives in Washington, for his encouragement, and for reading the manuscript in both its first and second drafts.

Dr. Frederick Drake, Professor of History at Brock University, and Past-President, *Hamilton-Scourge* Society, kindly read the manuscript and made useful suggestions regarding it, as did Dr. Kenneth McNaught, Professor of History, University of Toronto, and author of the *Pelican History of Canada*, Barry Lord, Chief Curator, Wentworth Pioneer Village, and my husband, Dr. Thomas Cain, Professor of English at McMaster University. In addition, he and our son Patrick took over my share of responsibility for our household during the writing of this book, all royalties from the sales of which go to the *Hamilton-Scourge* Project.

The *Hamilton-Scourge* Project, by its nature, elicits generous support and contributions. Among the institutions that have waived or lowered their fees or whose personnel have been particularly generous with time and energy in regard to this book are: the National Geographic Society; the Canada Centre for Inland Waters; the Royal Ontario Museum; the National Maritime Museum at Greenwich; the Public Archives of Canada; the Canadian War Museum; the Navy and Old Army Branch, National Archives; the Naval Historical Center, Department of the Navy; the Royal Military College of Canada; the McCord Museum; the Ontario Archives; the Essex Institute; the Peabody Museum; Sackets Harbor Battlefield State Historic Site; the Marine Museum of the Great Lakes; Turkstra Partners; Avenue Studios of Stelco, Inc. (Steel Company of Canada); the Oswego Public Library; the Metropolitan Library of Toronto; the Niagara Historical Society, the Regional Municipality of Hamilton-Wentworth; the City of Hamilton, particularly the Public Library's Special Collections, and the *Hamilton and Scourge* Foundation, Inc.

The National Geographic Society team put in many overtime hours while taking the underwater pictures of *Hamilton* and *Scourge* published in this book. Emory Kristof's beautiful photographs were made possible by his own extensive technical knowledge, but also by inventor and designer Chris Nicholson and his underwater vehicle built by Benthos, Inc., of Falmouth, Massachusetts. Back-up crew included Alvin M. Chandler, National Geographic special project engineer, and Geographic's electronics magician Mike Cole, Benthos technician Martin Bowen, Captain Ralph Tucker of Evan McKeil's tug *Lac Erie* and his crew, and archaeologist Holly Burch who shared with me the challenge of managing the galley. The survey was organized by Dr. Daniel A. Nelson, of St. Catharines, Ontario. All rights to the twenty-six hours of video-tape and approximately 1,900 slides taken at this time were given by the National Geographic Society to the *Hamilton-Scourge* Foundation.

The drawings for the endpapers of this book were donated by Ian Morgan, of Ships and Marine Canada. Among other individuals who have made generous contributions are: Syracuse newspaperman and author Richard Palmer, who supplied the primary documentation relating to *Diana*'s construction, and other valuable material; T. Melville Bailey, who loaned

Roy T. Woodhouse's file on the Crooks family; and Patricia Kennedy, Jeanne L'Espérance, and Donald Graves of the Public Archives of Canada. (The latter in particular supplied information concerning ordnance from his private files.) Dr. Robert Fraser of the *Dictionary of Canadian Biography*, University of Toronto, supplied the primary documentation for *Lord Nelson*'s construction at Niagara, Upper Canada, in 1811; Grace Crooks Leigh, by profession a librarian, but by avocation an author and family historian, who is a great grand-daughter of James Crooks and whose father settled the Crooks' case relative to *Lord Nelson*, provided the identity of the schooner's shipwright, the account of moneys expended in her building and outfitting, and her cargo list at the time of her capture.

I would also like to thank Brenda Brownlee, Curator of the Hamilton Military Museum, who generously made available many books from her private library; my mother, Isadore Smith (Ann Leighton), and her neighbour, Dana Story; William Booth, President, *Hamilton-Scourge* Society; model-makers Harold Hahn and Roger Cole; Christel Vanags; Harold and Dorothy Lampman; Martha Whittier, Oswego Public Library; Robert Markson of Sackets Harbor; Patrick Wilder, Interpretive Program Assistant, and Jesse Besaw, Historical Researcher, Sackets Harbor Battlefield State Historic Site; J.R. Gilbert; John Morand; Betty Mustard; Nina Chapple; Allison Gray; Ben Verburgh of the Ontario Science Centre; Captain Archie Hodge; Rosemary Nesbitt of the Oswego Maritime Museum; my sister-in-law Ellen Andersen of Widener Library; Mr. Ben Vanderbrug and his supportive staff of the Hamilton Region Conservation Authority; former Glaswegian Ena McCulloch; Dr. Peter Sly of the Canada Centre for Inland Waters; Anne Barrie, Assistant to the Director, Greenwich Maritime Museum; G.H. Cuthbertson, and Dr. William Dudley and his crew at the Naval Historical Center.

I would also like to thank the book's designer, my old friend and colleague, Peter Maher; Peggy McCarthy of Turkstra Partners; Ann Meema, City of Hamilton Legal Department and Ray Desjardins, City Traffic Commissioner, for work with contracts; and particularly E.A. Simpson, City Clerk, for the hospitality of his department, and for many kindnesses; Joseph Schatz, Secretary of the *Hamilton* and *Scourge* Foundation, Inc. and Committee, especially for sharing my friend and his secretary, Rosemary Warne, who spent several weekends putting this manuscript onto a word-processor, and did many other kind favours.

Emily Cain
Research and Co-ordinating Officer
Hamilton-Scourge Project
June, 1983

INDEX

Albany   19, 61, 62, 73
Amherstburg   89
American Army   59, 81, 92, 94, 118
American Revolution   21, 28
Angus, Lieutenant   79
Astor, John Jacob   39

Barclay, Captain James Heriot   89
Bass, George   128
Bathurst, Lord   79, 80
Battle of New Orleans   121
Battle of Stoney Creek   95
Battle of Waterloo   12, 59
Bay of Quinte   68
Bouchette, Joseph   20
British Army   26, 35, 64, 80, 85, 92, 93, 94, 118
Brock, Sir Issac   13, 59, 64, 121
Bronson, Alvin   38, 53, 54, 97
Brown Brothers   78
Buffalo Gazette   125
Burlington Heights, Upper Canada   97

Canada Act, 1791   12
Cartwright, Richard Jr.   53
Chauncey, Commodore Isaac   60, 61, 62, 63, 64, 65, 68, 70, 71, 72, 73, 76, 77, 78, 79, 81, 85, 88, 89, 90, 91, 92, 95, 96, 97, 98, 99, 100, 111, 112, 117, 118, 119, 125
Christensen, Borge Brorson   130
City of Hamilton   131
City of Hamilton Act, 1979   132
Clay, Henry   13, 59
Cleveland, President Grover   126
Clinton, De Witt   27, 37
Collins, Deputy Surveyor   24
Confederation   121
Conradsen, Hartvig   130
Cooper, James Fenimore   37, 38, 53, 61
Cornwallis, General   12
Cousteau, Jacques   128, 132
Crooks, Francis   26, 36
Crooks, Jane Cummings   36
Crooks, Honourable James   22, 36, 53, 55, 65, 125
Crooks, William   36, 65, 125
Crookston   36

Darragh, Alexander   56
Dearborn, General   81
Decatur, Stephen   118
Dennis, John   76
Devil's Nose   26
Dorchester, Lord   24

Eagle, Henry   39, 40, 63
Earle, Lieutenant Hugh   59, 60
East India Trade   37
Eckford, Henry   38, 39, 40, 61, 63
Elmer, Lieutenant F.   21
Embargo Act of 1807   13, 38
Embargo Act of 1812   54
Essex, Mass.   41, 46, 52

Falco, Albert   124, 132
Fenwick, Lieutenant Colonel   57
Fort Detroit   59, 77, 118
Fort Erie   34
Fort George   33, 65, 81, 85, 90, 92
Fort Malden   77
Fort Niagara   34, 36, 53, 88
Forty Mile Creek   95, 110, 125
Four Mile Creek   21

Gagnon, Emile   128
Genesee River   24, 54, 96, 117
Gray, Andrew   76
Great Sodus, New York   96, 97
Green, Lieutenant M.L.   89

Halifax   20, 73
Hamilton and *Scourge* Foundation, Inc.   132
Hamilton, Paul   53, 60, 63, 65, 68, 73
Hamilton, Robert   28, 35
Hamilton Region Conservation Authority   133
Hamilton-Scourge Project   130, 132
Hamilton-Scourge Society   132
Harrison, William Henry   77, 118
Head-of-the-Lake, Upper Canada   20, 36
Heriot, George   22, 27, 28, 29, 30, 32, 35
Hodge, Captain Archie   131
Hudson River   19
Huginin, Daniel   40
Huginin Family   40

Inland Navigation Act, 1788   24

Jackson, Andrew   121
Jarvis, Hannah Peters   23
Jarvis, William   23, 32, 56
Jay's Treaty   12, 21
Jefferson, Thomas   77
Johnson, John   55
Jones, William   76, 77, 78

Kingston   23, 27, 28, 29, 30, 31, 34, 36, 39, 53, 59, 68, 70, 71, 72, 73, 76, 81, 89, 93, 97, 99
Kingston Gazette   68
Kristof, Emory   132

McCormick, Augusta Honoria Jarvis   56
McCormick, Thomas   56
McCormick, Mrs.   56, 57, 63, 79, 88, 119
McCulloch, William M.   131
McDonald, John A.   131
Macdonough, Thomas   121
McKee, Alexander   130
McNair, Matthew   40
Macpherson, Lieutenant   68, 90, 92, 97
Madison, President James   59, 118
Mary Rose Committee   130
Maude, John   34
Michilimackinac   59, 64, 77, 120
Mohawk River   19
Montreal   19, 29, 30, 34, 73, 78, 89, 120
Monroe, President James   126
Myers, Ned   61, 62, 63, 66, 68, 72, 73, 81, 85, 88, 91, 99, 100, 101, 130

Napoleon Bonaparte   13, 58, 121
Napoleonic Wars   12, 40
National Geographic Society   132
National Museum of Denmark   130
Nelson, Daniel A.   130
Nelson, Lord   13
Newark, Upper Canada   32, 53, 54, 90
Niagara   20, 21, 23, 29, 32, 33, 34, 36, 71, 97, 99, 112, 125
Niagara Falls   19, 35, 53
Niagara-on-the-Lake   32
Niagara Peninsula   92, 95, 119, 120
Niagara River   19, 20, 26, 32, 33, 54, 64, 90, 131
Nicholson, Chris   132

Osgood, Sailing Master   61, 64, 90, 98, 100, 101, 105, 108, 110, 125
Oswego   21, 22, 27, 36, 37, 38, 39, 40, 55, 62, 63, 64, 73, 88, 96, 119
Oswego River   19

Perry, Oliver Hazard   78, 89, 90, 92, 118
Peters, Samuel   23
Pike, Zebulon   85
Portage Road   34, 36
Prescott   55
Prevost, Sir George   64, 76, 79, 80, 93, 95, 99, 110, 116
Provincial Marine Department   29, 38, 59, 60, 76, 79

Queen's Rangers   20
Queenston   33, 34, 35, 53, 56, 63, 64, 92

Record, George   76
Richardson, James   117

Royal Ontario Museum   130, 131-132
Roskilde Fjord   130
Rule, Margaret   130
Rush-Bagot Convention   121

Sacket, Augustus   53
Sackets Harbour   39, 53, 55, 59, 60, 61, 63, 65, 73, 77, 79, 81, 88, 89, 92, 93, 94, 96, 117
St. Lawrence River   19, 20, 28, 30, 33, 34, 54, 75
Sheaffe, Sir Roger Hale   85
Simcoe, Mrs. Elizabeth   20, 22, 26, 35
Simcoe, Colonel John Graves   20, 23, 28, 59
Skjelborg, Aage   130
Sly, Dr. Peter   130
Snider, C.H.J.   127
Story, A. D.   47
Swedish Museum of Maritime History   128

Tariff Act, 1789   12
Tecumseh   118
Tompkins, Daniel D.   62
Trant, Sailing Master James   90, 109, 110
Treaty of Ghent   13, 121
Treaty of Paris   12
Treaty of Versailles   20
Tushingham, Dr. A. Douglas   130

United Empire Loyalists   21, 23, 59, 70
United States Congress   79, 131

Vaughan, Madam   60
Vaughan, William   21
Vessels:
  Asp   88, 90
  Beaver   39
  Beresford   89, 93, 95, 96
  Bluenose I   41, 52
  Charles and Ann   53, 65, 97
  Columbia   41-52
  Conquest   66, 70, 88
  Constitution   60
  Diana (Hamilton)   27, 40, 41, 52, 53, 65, 66, 68, 70, 72, 73, 81, 88, 90, 92, 97, 98, 110, 112, 116, 124, 125, 127, 131, 132, 133
  Duke of Gloucester   30, 60, 65, 85, 88
  Durham Boat   34
  Earl of Moira   30, 60, 65, 72, 76, 89, 93
  Fair American   55, 64, 71, 88, 97
  Fly   96
  General Pike   71, 79, 92, 95, 97, 116, 117
  Genesee   27
  Governor Simcoe   65, 70, 89
  Governor Tompkins   65, 66, 70, 75, 88, 90, 97, 98, 110
  Growler   66, 70, 88, 90, 112, 116
  Julia   66, 70, 71, 88, 90, 109, 112, 116
  Kentucky Boat   34

Lark 96
Lord Nelson (Scourge) 22, 36, 40, 41, 52, 53, 54, 55, 56, 59, 63, 64, 65, 67, 71, 72, 73, 79, 81, 85, 88, 90, 97, 98, 100, 109, 110, 112, 116, 121, 125, 126, 127, 131, 132, 133

Madison 63, 71, 81, 88, 89, 90, 116, 117
Mary Hatt 54
Mary Rose 130, 133
Melville 96
Nancy 121

Oneida 38, 39, 53, 54, 55, 56, 59, 60, 63, 64, 66, 67, 69, 81, 88, 111, 116, 117
Ontario 54, 71, 88, 90
Peggy 40
Pert 66, 71, 88
Polly 27
Prince Regent 60, 65, 89
Psyche 75
Queen Margrethe's ship 130
Raven 88
Royal George 30, 60, 65, 67, 68, 69, 72, 89, 93
Seneca 66
Governor Simcoe 70, 72
Sir Issac Brock 76, 85
Sir Sidney Smith 93, 95
Soucoupe 124, 132
Southampton 80
Wasa 129, 133
Wolfe 76, 89, 93, 95, 99, 110, 116, 117, 130
York 26

War of 1812 12, 19, 22, 23, 24, 28, 59, 125
Washington, D.C. 38, 120
Washington, George 12
Weld, Isaac 24, 26, 29
Wellington, Arthur Wellesley 59
Willcocks, Joseph 28
Wilson, Alexander 37
Wingfield, David 72, 80, 93, 94
Winter, Lieutenant Walter 97, 98, 110, 125
Woolsey, Melancthon T. 38, 39, 53, 54, 56, 57, 60, 63, 72, 79, 88, 96, 125

Yeo, Sir James Lucas 72, 79, 81, 89, 93, 95, 96, 97, 99, 100, 111, 112, 116, 117, 119
York 20, 28, 29, 36, 81, 85, 97, 100, 106, 110, 116, 120
York (Toronto) Harbour 20, 117